54

Dancing in Poppies

Dancing in Poppies

by
Gail Bowen & Ron Marken

Introduction by
Mary Blackstone

Canadian Plains Research Center, 2002

Canadian Plains Research Center
University of Regina
Regina, Saskatchewan   S4S 0A2
Canada
Tel: (306) 585-4795
Fax: (306) 585-4699
e-mail: canadian.plains@uregina.ca
http://www.cprc.ca

National Library of Canada Cataloguing in Publication Data

Bowen, Gail, 1942–
  Dancing in poppies

(University of Regina publications, ISSN 1480-0004 ; 8)
A play.
Based on: Bowen, Gail, 1942–   1919, the love letters of George and
        Adelaide.
Includes bibliographical references.
ISBN 0-88977-143-X

1. Canada—History1918–1939—Drama. I. Marken, Ron, 1939–
II. University of Regina. Canadian Plains Research Center.
III. Bowen, Gail, 1942–   1919, the love letters of George and
Adelaide. IV. Title. V. Series. PS8553.O8995D36 2002   C812'.54
C2002-910993-0   PR9199.3.B629D36 2002

Printed and bound in Canada by Houghton Boston, Saskatoon
Cover design by Donna Achtzehner, Canadian Plains Research Center

CONTENTS

Introduction

The Development of *Dancing in Poppies*

> *Nothing has a beginning. There is no first moment. You can point to no solitary word, no shaft of light across the path and say, "There ... that's where it started." Threads can be traced. They can be followed back into earlier stories. You will always find scraps and tissues of former reports. Within every tale that begins "Once upon a time," there is an infinite number of stories, each with its own "Once" and its own "time." So ... where we begin is arbitrary, perhaps even whimsical.* (1)

The observation by Roger at the opening of *Dancing in Poppies* applies as much to the evolution of this play as it does to the world he conjures up. The seeds of the play can be traced back to an initial collaboration between Gail Bowen and Ron Marken in conjunction with the satirical collection, *The Easterners' Guide to Western Canada* (1985) for which Bowen (under the name of Hildy Rhodes) wrote a letter from a private school girl transplanted to Saskatchewan about a belly-bumping contest. This letter inspired the publisher to suggest that Marken and Bowen collaborate on a further epistolary project involving East-West perspectives which resulted in the novella, *1919: The Love Letters of George and Adelaide* (1987). Having chosen the year 1919 to a large extent because neither writer knew much about the world events or social context for that particular year, Bowen and Marken undertook considerable period research for the novella. They listened to music of the period, looked at pictures, read literature about the war period and generally tried to immerse themselves in the world of the play. Marken recalls that inspiration came in part from photos and medals connected with his wife's uncle who lied about his age and was killed in World War I, but Marken pursued his research further. The war stories in the letters and the play are not imagined, but rather they are based on first-hand accounts of men and women he interviewed as part of his research.

Despite this preparation, however, the epistolary format of the piece evolved simply and naturally without a great deal of prior planning. They agreed the letters would run for one year from October 1918 to

October 1919, and they flipped a coin to determine who would start. Their writing process involved literally exchanging letters (Bowen's were actually handwritten) between Regina and Saskatoon via STC bus. Initially, Ron wrote George's letters and Gail wrote from the point of view of Adelaide and Roger, but it eventually became clear that such strict division of labour would not yield a polished work of fiction. Only later through the editing process were the letters given the shape and structure of a novella, and Bowen credits this process with teaching her that "when you begin a project you need to know where you're going."

Three years after the publication of *1919*, Susan Ferley, then Artistic Director of the Globe Theatre in Regina, was contemplating a Valentine's Day fundraiser for the Theatre and looking for something that could be presented in the form of a rehearsed reading augmented by champagne and chocolate. Globe General Manager, Victor Geridens, drew her attention to the novella and although the Valentine's Day project ultimately never came to pass, Ferley decided to commission Bowen and Marken to adapt their novella for the stage. From the Globe's early days it had made a strong commitment to the development of new work and under Ken Kramer's tenure it had been the first Canadian theatre to employ a full-time playwright-in-residence. The serious financial challenges facing the theatre when Ferley took up the position of Artistic Director led her to set aside this commitment, but by the end of the 1990–91 season Ferley had cleared the deficit. Recognizing that her audience had been accustomed to seeing premiers of new Saskatchewan work, she renewed this commitment before the end of her first season with the theatre.

Ferley's recollection of her decision to commission the stage adaptation is that "it just felt right," but within the context of the theatre's recent financial problems the decision required a considerable leap of faith. In form and texture the epistolary novella would require substantial adaptation if it were to succeed on the stage. One of the two co-authors had never written for the stage, and the novella had in fact been her first work of fiction. As well, the Theatre lacked any staff besides Ferley who could guide the developmental process, so it would be necessary for her to not only assemble a new team of people to contribute to that process but also develop from scratch a particular approach which would serve the writers and the play effectively. The result of this leap of faith, however, was regarded by all involved—from playwrights to director to the Globe's various audiences—as a success, and it is therefore worthy of some elaboration for those interested more generally in new play development.

To begin with, Ferley, who was not only the Globe's Artistic Director but also the eventual director of the premiere, made a strong commitment to producing the play and assumed the central, organizing role in the play's development from the point of commissioning through to the opening night. From the beginning it was clear that the subject matter had a particular resonance for her: "My father fought in World War II, and the insistence that we not forget was an important part of my growing up. We have to remember the human cost when we go into armed conflict." In her letter to Prince Edward in September of 1994 following the visit which occasioned a performance of an abbreviated version of the play, Ferley confides that she is "deeply attached to the play for many professional and personal reasons," and speaking nine years after the play's premier, having recently chosen it for the 2002–03 season at the Grand Theatre in London, Ontario, Ferley remarked that "the humanity of the piece continues to move me. I still feel transformed by its journey out of darkness to a celebration of the beauty of life's dance."

Once Bowen and Marken had the beginnings of their script (a first draft of Act I), Ferley began assembling a diverse team of people who would support the writers as they worked. Early participants included myself as dramaturg, choreographer Christine Trapp, sound designer Rob Bryanton, and actors Kent Allen, Burgandy Code, Paula Costain, Kelly Handerek and Tom Rooney. Ferley was fortunate to be able to draw on these actors, most of whom had significant experience with new play development, especially through workshops organized by the Saskatchewan Playwrights Centre. The process was never fraught with tension due to pressure to rush the development (except when we got to the first week of rehearsal without an ending for the play). Ferley gave the play time to evolve over the 1991–92 season through a series of workshops followed by the exchange of notes and revisions, and although Ferley was an active participant in the feedback process, her vision in no way dominated. Many of the workshops in which she had been involved in the past had lent themselves to strong actors creating strong roles, but Ferley wanted to create an environment in which participants were focused on serving the writers' vision and creating a strong play.

Development proceeded in a spirit of openness and collaboration that facilitated the discovery of what each participant had to contribute to the play regardless of designated titles such as playwright, dramaturg or actor. This may have had something to with the fact that we were dealing with an adaptation for which there was a common source which could stand as a point of reference for all participants, but it also had to do with the synergy between what the play needed and what the developmental team had to offer. For instance, Burgandy Code's beautiful singing voice inspired the inclusion of more and more music and the discovery that this music could provide valuable links and transitions between scenes. My own interest in vocal music from this era enabled me to suggest appropriate songs and make them available to the writers and the development team. In the context of workshop discussion, Kelly Handerek shared a personal memory of the harmonica which he cherished as a reminder of his father and his service in World War II. When discussion turned to possible titles for the play, it was also Handerek who suggested a paraphrase of the line from the play, "A girl in a red dress, dancing in a field of poppies."

The fact that many of these discoveries and contributions made their way into the final draft of the play had much to do with the attitude that the playwrights brought to the process and their own openness to collaborative discovery. Marken recalls that the workshop process "taught me that *Dancing in Poppies* isn't just our play—it really belongs to the collective. We gave one element to the process, but the others teased and encouraged things out of us." Both Marken and Bowen credit the workshops as contributing to the development of not only the play but also their skill as playwrights. Although some directors or dramaturgs might have simply provided verbal or written feedback on the first draft of the play, Ferley and I provided little feedback to the writers before taking that draft directly to a professional reading and workshop in July of 1991. Today Marken and Bowen consider that first workshop to have been an invaluable investment, although at the time the process was painful. Bowen, in particular, had had little contact with the creative side of theatre beyond attendance at plays and teaching them as literature to university students. It was her first opportunity to hear her work read by actors, and she recalls initially approaching the play as "words on a page" and the actors as "empty vessels to fill." Listening to Roger's initial monologue (which was considerably longer in the first draft than it is now), both Bowen and Marken observed the other actors sitting idly by and realized that they were not making the best use of what theatre had to offer. When Ferley moved the workshop from the table to actor improvisations based on the characters and actions described in Roger's monologue and Bowen saw Code knitting and intuitively interpolating the character which she had only just encountered, Bowen learned what actors could bring to the process and realized that they "came at truth from a different direction." Both writers agree that after the first workshop they understood much better how to proceed than they would have understood from dramaturg or director notes, and they came away with a much greater respect for what others could contribute to the realization of their play.

There were in total five workshops leading up to the rehearsal process, each one quite different in focus and format depending on the nature of the most recent draft. Early workshops encouraged the playwrights to spend some time articulating what the play was about, and all participants were involved in trying to tell the story of the play as clearly and simply as possible. An early part of the process, however, also involved taking the play away from table discussion and getting the actors up on their feet. Because of the play's roots in a novella dependent on words, description and epistolary monologue, Ferley used verbing to explore the essential actions connected with character and scene, and she introduced physical exercises to experiment with what the actors could communicate through movement. The introduction of a choreographer, a set designer and a sound designer helped the writers develop a sense of how to shift some of the responsibility from telling to showing. Encouraging the entire team to respond to the play with personal stories also helped the writers understand the emotional world opened up by the play and the potential response of the audience.

As dramaturg, my primary concerns were character consistency and complexity, and plot structure within the conventions which were appropriate to the playwrights' vision of the play. I prepared questions (usually not for the writers but for the other participants) and observations for the workshops, and I took copious notes within the workshops. After the workshop these were compiled with more of my own observations and questions and provided in written form to the writers and the director. I made no attempt to follow the chronology of the workshop but rather attempted to create a useful working document organized around topics such as character, dialogue or plot structure or according to the chronology of lines and scenes in the play. These notes were followed up by consultations involving writers and/or director outside the workshops. The major dramaturgical challenge in developing this adaptation was overcoming the constant pull of the narrative source in favour of a more dramatic structure. The fact that the playwrights decided early in the process that the novella would simply be a starting point and that story and character would change as needed to create an effective stage piece helped considerably in achieving the transition to drama, but the challenges of shaping endings for both acts remained, and the introduction of Roger as a central figure—both as Adelaide's first love interest and the frame for the drama—created further challenges. Large portions of *1919* were jettisoned, George and Adelaide became increasingly independent as characters, and it became necessary to develop a throughline for Roger even after his suicide at the end of the first act.

The interjection of Roger proved to be a destabilizing force throughout the development process. To paraphrase film theorist Rick Altman, Roger questions and challenges "the social, political and cultural machine" (p. 6). He resists the hegemonic construction of social structures and the roles, beliefs and values expected of his generation. This resistance drives the play even after his death when George and Adelaide struggle to move beyond it to alternative constructions of their own. Likewise Roger proved to be a destabilizing force within the dramaturgical form and structure conceived by the writers. Serving as a useful developmental, process-based footnote to Ric Knowles' recent book, *The Theatre of Form and the*

Production of Meaning: Contemporary Canadian Dramaturgies, Roger defies the conventions of time and space linked to the otherwise traditional form and structure of the play (pp. 19–20 and *passim*). Containing the negativity of Roger's words with vision and action was necessary to achieve the playwrights' concept, but the ongoing challenges of developing his throughline and revising the endings of both acts were a measure of the difficulty with which Roger and what he represents was contained.

Fortunately, Bowen and Marken had learned with *1919* that revisions are an important part of the writing process. In response to their editor's criticisms, Bowen apparently protested that the novella was not "supposed to be *War and Peace*. It's just something to put in your aunt's Christmas stocking," to which the editor replied, "If you're going to put it in her stocking, you better give her something good to read too." She admits that it is not easy to be criticized and revise, but you have to learn to "keep your ego out of the process. This isn't you. This is a piece of paper. You have to be tough and learn to take criticism. Everyone involved in the process wants it [your writing] to be as good as it can be." This is especially true of theatre, which she regards as genuinely collaborative in producing the creative work which the audience experiences, whereas this really isn't true in either fiction or screenwriting. In fiction, the editor may push you, but you push back and ultimately the decisions and what engages the reader are your own. In screenwriting the writer is too insignificant in the overall process to have a genuine sense of collaboration.

When rehearsals began in January of 1993, Bowen recalls the first reading of the play and the presentation of the design for Adelaide's red dress by costume designer Russell Danielson as more exciting than opening night. My own recollection of the first read-through is of both anxiety and surprise—anxiety because I knew we still did not have a workable ending for the play and surprise that even after the lengthy involvement in the practicalities of putting the play together the first reading could move me as it did. It was during the first week of rehearsals that Bowen and I locked ourselves in Ferley's office until we could emerge with the final act as it was premiered in 1993, but at the same time we made a note of changes that were made under pressure and that we would like to revisit if the play were to be published or given a second production. Bowen notes that she has never felt the urge to revise any of her published fiction, but this play was different. Too few Canadian plays receive this second chance, but fortunately this edition has benefited from the play's second life at the Grand Theatre in 2002.

Neither writer attended further rehearsals, and although Marken observed that it might have been interesting to attend a rehearsal, it is a measure of the development process leading up to the rehearsals that both writers expressed "complete confidence in Susan" to realize the play as they had intended. Both felt that it was time "to let others do their job." This confidence proved to be well founded. Ferley's comfort with the play and the involvement of two of the three actors in the workshop process enabled her to spend time on things like a lengthy discussion of images and metaphors which could help the cast ground the play outside of the narrative frame, but Ferley's involvement in the developmental process also presented her with different challenges. She was concerned about "getting to the end of the rehearsal process too soon—without the journey." This was especially a concern for Mike Stack who played the complex and pivotal role of Roger and who had not been involved in the developmental process. As dramaturg I attended some rehearsals and provided responses to the director's queries as well as potential audience and playwright response. Ferley also brought interested members of the public into the rehearsal process—for instance, an individual from the Canadian National Institute for the Blind and a policeman trained in military behaviour.

On opening night both writers reported being excited rather than nervous because they had developed a trust in both Susan and the actors and a confidence that the play would be well received. In a preview article for the *Leader-Post*, Bowen revealed, "I'm nervous when it's my books, where your ego is out there and so attached [to the work]. This play, all of us did it. ... I want to see what everyone else is doing [with it]." (Pilon, "A Whole New Way to Write") Both writers liked what they saw— although Bowen recalls spending as much time watching the audience responding to the play as she did watching the play itself. For Marken it was first of all a relief for him and his family to simply be in the theatre. Leaving Saskatoon for Regina just after his wife had finished work, the family had gotten a close encounter with the realities of Saskatchewan geography and climate that figure prominently in the play. Traveling in –25°C temperatures, their car died nearly an hour outside of Regina. In the end they arrived in the city via a tow truck and roared up to the theatre just a few minutes before the show started. Despite this, he recalls that "the family was bowled over by the imaginative use of space" and the convincing way in which geographical distances were evoked. He will never forget the impressive effect of lighting the match and the growing sense that "the audience was with us all the way."

The results of this development process extended beyond the successful run of the play. Marken had been involved in a workshop for his earlier play, *Flights of Angels*, but he admits that he had too much personal and emotional investment in that play to really benefit from that workshop. But with *Dancing in Poppies* Marken talks about "these unbelievable workshops," "weekends with many people" where he really began to understand how the collaborative dimension of theatre can work. Bowen credits the workshops with inspiring a continuing interest in playwriting and improving her skills not only as a playwright but also as a writer of fiction: "There was a huge change in my fiction between the first three books (written before *Dancing in Poppies*) and the later books. I moved to a much cleaner, less cluttered writing style." She also found that a concern for playable action in each scene could be usefully transferred to her fiction. For the theatre, *Dancing in Poppies* rekindled a commitment to the development of new work, which at that time hung in the balance, while moving it in a somewhat different direction with respect to process and approach. It also paved the way for the development of more new plays at the Globe during Ferley's tenure including three more plays by Gail Bowen, *The Great Electrical Revolution* by Ken Mitchell, and *Speak* by Greg Nelson. The latter was commissioned and produced by the Globe but developed and given its premiere by Alberta Theatre Projects.

The Premiere and Other Productions

Dancing in Poppies premiered at Regina's Globe Theatre on February 18, 1993 with the cast and company listed elsewhere in this edition. It opened to a standing ovation from an audience of about 375 and enjoyed a very successful run of three weeks. *Leader-Post* reviewer, Bernard Pilon, called it an "excellent drama"— "funny, poignant, touching" and "another in a continuing series of Globe winners" under Ferley's direction. Opening night was especially moving because of strong attendance by numerous war veterans for whom the play had special meaning, but as observed by Pilon, the play seemed to speak more broadly as "a wake-up call to those of us too absorbed in destructive self-pity and navel-gazing to shake off life's injustices and move on" and more specifically as "an inspiration to the Saskatchewan youth of today—a generation unsure about the wisdom of taking over the family farm, teens wondering if they'll ever find a decent job in a recession that refuses to end." (Pilon, "A Wake-up Call about the Power of Change")

The play was performed in the round on the Globe's main stage using a revolve with a simple set design which used a limited amount of furniture and props to evoke period and places. The production relied heavily on original music and the sound and lighting design to effect fluid transitions between places and sections of the play. Projections against the walls of the theatre were used in particular to enhance the experience of the cross-Canada tour in Act II. The costumes further developed the period texture of the production, and the predominantly muted colours made Adelaide's red dress all the more striking a statement. Under Ferley's direction, each of these elements combined with the acting to create an effect which began by acknowledging the roots of the play in an epistolary novella (including the reading and writing of letters on different parts of the stage) but which ultimately swept the audience up in the action and

Susan Ferley at the Premiere, February 18, 1993

interaction of the dramatic dancing metaphor and literally took them from darkness in the opening scene to the brilliant light with which the play ends.

In March of 1992, the Globe Theatre announced that His Royal Highness The Prince Edward had bestowed the honour of royal patronage on the theatre. It was at that time the first and only royal patronage granted by Prince Edward in Canada, and from the beginning it was perceived as an opportunity to host the new patron for a royal gala at the theatre. The visit was eventually scheduled for August 14, 1994 at the beginning of a longer tour of western Canada which culminated in his attendance at the XV Commonwealth Games in Vancouver. Billed as a "working visit" rather than an "official visit," the Prince's itinerary within the limited length of his stopover allowed him to see at most a one-hour performance on the Globe's stage. Visits to a sea cadet training facility, a drug and alcohol rehabilitation facility and a powwow attended by 6,000 Dakotah Sioux at Standing Buffalo Indian Reserve near Fort Qu'Appelle preceded an official opening ceremony for the Scarth Street Mall (on which the Globe Theatre is situated) and the gala performance. These festivities were followed the next day by an award ceremony, a fundraising luncheon, a visit to the RCMP training academy and an official dinner.

For this occasion Ferley wanted to profile the work of Saskatchewan writers, and it made sense to choose the first new play developed during her tenure as well as a proven stage success which just happened to feature the Canadian tour of another British prince. Because the production was being prepared for a fall provincial tour as well, the choice of *Dancing in Poppies* also made practical and financial sense. The one-hour format was the problem, however. With a director's eye as to what she could accomplish within one hour of stage time and what might play well before her distinguished guest, she undertook a radical adaptation of the play which was approved by the playwrights. The adaptation reduced the development of the Roger-Adelaide-George relationship in Toronto and cut many accounts of other men at the hospital as well as descriptions of war experiences overseas. Events which Adelaide described as happening to her in Toronto were greatly streamlined, including the development of her career as a journalist and her scenes with Ben. Both Toronto and Saskatoon scenes marking the armistice were reduced to a few lines plus special effects (some of which failed to materialize in the actual performance). Adelaide and George were allowed comparatively few lines in immediate response to Roger's suicide, and overall, many of Roger's more caustic lines were dropped. The character of Jack and much of George's scenes in Winnipeg and at University were cut, as were Adelaide's stops in Halifax and Saskatoon. The result was an emphasis on the Toronto, Calgary and Vancouver portions of the Prince's tour and overall a greater profile for the George and Adelaide love story over the Roger-Adelaide attraction and disillusionment with the war. Ironically, Ferley cut the section of the original Scene 19 in which Adelaide's description of events most closely paralleled Prince Edward's experience earlier in the day of his visit:

> *Today the Prince became Chief Morning Star. At the Banff train station we were met by men from the Stoney nation. They were on horseback and they formed a kind of escort for the Prince. As our cavalcade wound down the mountain roads to the valley, more and more of the Stoney people fell in behind us.*
>
> *When we came to the valley, everything was still.*
>
> *Then, the drums began, and the people began to dance: first the men and the boys, then the women and the girls, until the whole valley was alive with the pounding of the dancers' feet and the beat of the drums. And then—I don't know how to explain it, I lost the sense that I was Adelaide Farlinger. The sounds of the dancing and drumming were bouncing off the sides of the mountains and back down into the valley, and it seemed as if the whole valley were a drum and I was inside it. Faster and louder and faster and louder and then suddenly—silence.*

> *I felt more tired than I can ever remember feeling—and drained, as if everything inside me was gone and I was just a shell. And then I felt a hand in mine—warm and very dry, like leaves in the autumn sun—and I turned and I was looking into the face of an old woman from the Stoney tribe. Her face was seamed with age but her eyes were a young person's eyes, bright an searching. She spoke very slowly and her voice was so soft. But George, I did not mistake her words.*

> *(ROGER speaks the old woman's words.)*

> *"It's good that you let your friend go on his journey. He was ready."*

I have cited this scene fully because the passage has also been cut from the final draft of the play as published in this edition—largely because the writers regarded it as creating the effect of a false ending without sufficient connection with the rest of the text. Initially it was included in the performed script because it brought in another dimension of the Canadian dynamic and because one of the key lessons that Adelaide must learn is the need to let go of the dead, wisdom that is central to Aboriginal beliefs and spiritual practice. Written before the planned visit of the Prince, however, this passage is also interesting not only because of the extent to which it foreshadows Prince Edward's reception at a powwow but also because it parallels journalists' accounts from a supposedly "post colonial" era of how such colonial rituals continue to carry meaning for the participants. (See Bell and Sutter, "Prince Tastes Native Culture.")

The royal gala was attended by 400 guests including federal, provincial and civic officials, the Globe's Board of Directors, corporate sponsors, individual donors and subscribers. It began with a reception so that many of the audience members had met the Prince by the time they settled into their seats for the play. The politics of Regina's theatre in-the-round (Canada's first professional theatre to be so configured) led to interesting dynamics as without a royal box or traditional "front seats" the Prince was nestled in amongst all the other members of the audience and his response to the production was as much part of the performance as what happened on stage. This was especially so for the playwrights who were seated directly across from the Prince. After the show they enjoyed more personal and extended contact with the Prince when he was guest of honour at an informal buffet which included not only the Globe Board but also the playwrights and all of the staff that worked at the theatre.

All reports of the gala performance, including the official August 22 letter of thanks from Buckingham Palace, describe it as "a great success and superbly performed." The Prince stayed at the theatre for more than an hour longer than laid out in his itinerary, and in a *Leader-Post* article the day after the Prince's departure, Irene Janz, a senior provincial protocol

His Royal Highness The Prince Edward, at the royal gala, August 14, 1994

officer, identifies the Globe gala as the highlight of the visit for the Prince: "He was obviously in his element and enjoying himself immensely." (O'Connor)

From its inception in 1966 as a school touring company the Globe Theatre had maintained a strong touring tradition. Although financial realities also threatened this tradition early in Ferley's tenure, the success of *Dancing in Poppies* led Nan Carson of the Organization of Saskatchewan Arts Councils to encourage her to pursue a tour. Both felt that the play would speak to audiences in small Saskatchewan towns and give them an opportunity to see themselves on stage in a professional production with Saskatchewan roots. Local corporate sponsors (AgrEvo, Crown Life Insurance and the Saskatchewan Wheat Pool) agreed with them, and further contributions from the Canada Council Touring Office and the Saskatchewan Arts Board made the tour possible.

Consequently, in 1994 for the three and a half weeks leading up to Remembrance Day, *Dancing in Poppies* toured to 20 Saskatchewan towns and cities ranging in population from 193 to 15,500: Kindersley, Unity, the Battlefords, Nipawin, Tisdale, Hudson Bay, Preeceville, Wynyard, Canora, Yorkton, Langenburg, Redvers, Carnduff, Estevan, Assiniboia, Swift Current, Shaunavon, Kincaid, Weyburn and Kipling. Many of these communities were small and isolated with few opportunities to see professional theatre and limited facilities in which to present such a production. Performance venues included schools, legion halls, community and recreation centres as well as theatres and arts centres. The distances to be covered by the touring company (over 3,200 km in all) as well as variations in the size and technical facilities of venues represented the greatest challenges for the tour. Designer John Thompson and Ferley adapted the production from theatre-in-the-round to a flexible proscenium arch configuration which could expand or contract to make the best use of the performance spaces, which ranged from 16 to 40 feet in width. Ferley worked with the cast (which included a new actor, Marcel Jeannin, as Roger) so that they were prepared to open up or reduce the spatial demands of their performance depending on the venue and gave the actors an opportunity to try out their abilities to do this by taking the production to Regina's Darke Hall with its limited technical facilities and small proscenium arch stage. Beyond these modifications, however, neither the production nor the play changed significantly from the initial run in 1993.

As expected, the production proved highly successful with its provincial audience. The actors reported experiencing some of the most moving responses to a production in which they had been involved. They were humbled, for instance, by people who had lost sons or daughters through suicide approaching them after the show to thank them for the performance and ask for advice on how to deal with such a loss. Bowen, who attended the November 10 performance of the play in Weyburn, describes the show as memorable not simply because of the performance itself but also because of the way in which the audience and community became a part of it. When in the first scene Jeannin introduced himself ("By the way, I'm Roger Currie. How do you do?"), members of the audience responded, "Hi Roger!"—something that caught both actor and playwright off guard. Other individuals in the audience had come wearing their medals and uniforms. Bowen could see that "they knew what war is and they were really involved to the point of tears."

The Play

The play as printed here is not the version first performed by the Globe Theatre. This edition and the impending production of the play at the Grand Theatre in London, Ontario in October of 2002 inspired the playwrights to return to problematic sections of the play which could not be fully addressed prior to the premiere, to take a fresh look at the whole play with the benefit of time and a production history and to consider ways in which it could be made more flexible for wider audiences and different performance venues. In particular, throughlines for all three characters, especially Roger, have been strengthened in the second act and some attention has been paid to the extent to which scenes written for theatre-in-the-round will work in a proscenium arch space. Some specifically Saskatchewan references have been altered to situate the play in a broader, Canadian context.

Much of the play, however, has remained constant into this printed edition, and some sections, like Roger's opening speech, have in fact changed little from the very beginning of the development process. Roger's speech sets the tone for a play which is about beginnings on several levels. Marken has always been fascinated by how plays start. Paraphrasing from an eighteenth century publication, the author of which he has long forgotten but the sentiment of which had a major impact on the play, he observes that "before a play starts everything is possible, but with the first gesture or the first word or the first flash of light or the first thread of costume suddenly the possibilities are infinitely limited. That's what I had in mind at the beginning of this play. I … wrote my way out of darkness."

On one level then, the play is about the beginnings and new possibilities ironically created by the destructive and negative force of war. The play clearly condemns war by showing us what it does to young people: the Rogers and the Joes who cannot make it out of the abyss, and the Georges and Adelaides who struggle in the vacuum of its aftermath but find the strength to create a brighter future. It is perhaps a sad commentary on human nature that apart from causing us to reflect on a particular point in history, plays about war always have the potential to be fresh. Speaking of her choice to include the play in the Grand Theatre's 2002–03 season, Ferley observes that it will have an even "greater resonance now that troops are actually fighting," but the play is also more generally about the new beginnings which come with going home.

All three of the characters in the play are disillusioned by returning home. George and Roger and others like them return to Canada with nothing of the fanfare that sent them off to sacrifice their youth—little thanks and no jobs. Adelaide returns home from St. Andrew's hospital to a privileged family seeking to preserve its social and historical perspectives and deaf to the concerns of young people like herself:

> *All you young people live for is pleasure. You lack respect for God, the Monarchy, the Dominion and Your Elders. … We give the boys the adventure of war, and they come home and grouse about jobs. No spine. Convalescent hospitals full of them. "Nerve cases," they call themselves. Fakers, I call them. Rather lie about and be mollycoddled than go out and do a day's work. They're no better than the girls— pantywaists.* (28)

In this way, the play highlights a dynamic period in Canadian history —only partly precipitated by the war—when fixed social and political structures built on stereotypes of class, gender and ethnicity were beginning to crumble. The play situates its characters against a backdrop of internal struggles which were the beginnings of freedoms we take for granted today. Although motivated to turn away from this kind of confrontation, George is on hand for the Winnipeg General Strike and the beginnings of the labour movement. Addy insists on continuing her work at St. Andrew's, punches Uncle William in the nose in a symbolic confrontation with the older generation, and takes up working as a journalist for a Jewish editor despite pressure from her father to silence her. Thus, her entire character throughline dramatizes the increasing independence for women that can be traced back to the suffragette movement of the period.

Moreover, Adelaide's journey can be read as a coming of age story— a coming of age for not just one young woman, but also a generation of young people and a nation as a whole. In the initial production it was clear that the young people in *Dancing in Poppies* could connect with both older and younger generations. Ferley was conscious of how the play could reach out to not only older members of the audience who had lived through war or grown up in the aftermath of it, but also younger members of the audience "seeking, on so many fronts—a positive way to live." (Pilon, "A Canadian War Story.") In her Director's Notes for the program Ferley describes the play as being about "young people and a young country; about love and friendship; about asking questions and seeking answers; and about celebrating in the midst of darkness." The challenge in writing and producing this play has been in finding the balance between the questioning, the spiritual emptiness, negativity and cynicism which consume Roger and the positives of friendship, love and hope through which George and Adelaide eventually find a sense of direction, a purpose and a reason to celebrate. But this is the challenge experienced by many young people at the turn of the twenty-first century as well, and if there is to be a twenty-second century the balance has to tip in favour of Adelaide's "*Eiréne*" and her hope for the future. By the time Roger closes the play he has worked through the devaluation of the words that meant so much to him, through the spiritual despair generated by the war and through the pain he inadvertently inflicted on his friends to learn that, as Bowen has observed, "We can't just be defined by terrible things. We have to retain a sense that good is possible." Gradually through the characters he portrays Roger assumes a more positive influence and perspective. By helping his friends to find a sense of direction, some spiritual strength, he gives his own life and death meaning. As darkness threatens to bring the play to a close in the manner that it began, Roger turns it back to the audience with a challenge that has evolved over the course of the evening. As articulated by Pilon in his review, the play is ultimately "about empowerment, about channeling all that energy people use to bitch about this and that into a force for change." ("A Wake-up Call about the Power of Change.")

What is interesting in this play is that both Adelaide and George begin to find their sense of direction only when they travel the country and move away from their home bases in East and West. Through his journey from Snipe Lake to Winnipeg to Toronto, George comes to the conclusion, "If I'm going to make any changes, I'll have to do a lot of reading and a lot of learning." Similarly, it is really only after her trip across the country covering the Prince of Wales' tour that Adelaide is able to let go of Roger during her stop in Banff and embrace a sense of peace when she reaches Vancouver. Although the play had its roots in the East-West dichotomy which has characterized Canada since before it became a country, *Dancing in Poppies* has ultimately mitigated against such a dichotomy at several levels. Just as the characters journey from provincially bound perspectives to a broader vision of Canada as a whole, so too the writers who began this project with an intention to speak with distinctly eastern and western Canadian voices ultimately crossed over to write for all three characters and created a play which grapples with broader concerns which will not be confined within provincial dichotomies.

It has been observed that World War I initiated the disintegration of false boundaries of class and ethnicity, boundaries which to some degree have contributed to the East-West divide. After the war, Canada's coming of age as a country presumably involved a gradual evolution of national, as well as regional identity, but the history and evolution of Canadian theatre in the twentieth century are a testimony to the challenges of achieving such a vision. Today, the East-West divide, closely related to an urban-rural divide, is nowhere more evident than in the world of theatre. To conclude her Director's Notes in the program, Ferley underscores a defining dimension of theatre: "This play comes to life on stage with you —for you, the audience, are the final component in bringing this creation to life." As the most social of the art forms, theatre depends on references to the recognizable, the local, the particular to draw its audiences together within a live, shared experience, here and now. A sense of place—which is often both inclusive and exclusive—can be an important element in creating a shared response. For example, when George explains to Adelaide that "in Snipe Lake, we don't even have trees! You can see Rosetown from our farm … and that's fifty miles away," the Saskatchewan productions have always gotten a laugh. Similarly, when George reads,

> *Come my friends, 'tis not too late to seek a newer world*
> *…my purpose holds*
> *To sail beyond the sunset, and the baths*
> *Of all the western stars*
> *To seek … to find…,*

his conclusion, "I've always wanted to visit Winnipeg!," inevitably engenders laughter. Written with a distinctly Saskatchewan voice, *Dancing in Poppies* is a good example of how we define ourselves and discover who we are through theatre.

Part of the challenge, however, in revising the play with an Ontario production in the offing has been in gauging the extent to which its voice is distinctly Canadian. To what extent are its sense of place and the sensibilities connected with audiences in such a place portable to a different or broader Canadian context? In his review, Pilon identified "the strength of *Dancing in Poppies*" as "its ability to work on various levels," ("Wakeup Call about the Power of Change") and it was indeed the intention of the writers to create a work with both regional and national appeal. Marken draws a distinction between provincialism—which is narrow, exclusive and inward looking—and regionalism—which takes the character and personality of a place and makes it universal. He argues that "all great literature is regional—Homer, the Bible, Milton."

In Canadian theatre, however, the devolution of new plays tends to be governed by centrifugal force. They emanate from the centre to the regions and in so doing can be perceived as defining the national character of Canadian theatre. Comparatively few regional plays have bucked this trend or have even successfully transferred from one region to another. Speaking of new plays developed in Atlantic Canada, Denyse Lynde has drawn attention to the tendency for new plays and productions to be tied to "separate and discrete communities" and even when they are published "they remain unknown and unread" (p. 247). Canadian dramaturg, D.D. Kugler has suggested that "there's a lot of Saskatchewan work that I think would play well in Toronto if it weren't seen as regional work. That's part of the problem. The work is prejudged through a particular lens without considering what it could say to an audience in Toronto" (pp. 95–96).

The Canadian coming of age depicted in this play, however, can only be fully realized when more plays like *Dancing in Poppies* reverse this trend. Marken has observed that "the play has a birthplace in Snipe Lake, Saskatchewan, which is misunderstood, misrepresented and mocked. In a country like Canada that's not good enough." With this publication it is hoped that the play will reach a wider audience through classrooms and community theatres as well as professional theatres. Although speaking from the geographical margins, this play asks recurring questions and concerns itself with war, disillusionment, ideals, love, despair and hope. Scholars such as Robert Wallace in his book *Producing Marginality: Theatre and Criticism in Canada*, have quite rightly thrown into question the extent to which the commonality of universals is possible or even desirable in postmodern Canadian theatre where he suggests the trend is towards more particularized audiences and theatres. Arguably, though, plays like *Dancing in Poppies* can provide a cultural touchstone which is as necessary for the social medium of theatre as it is to the fabric of a country. To paraphrase Robert Lecker, who has applied Charles Altieri's theory of "cultural grammar" to Canadian literature, this play has the potential to have ongoing impact over time; its "cultural grammar" is both local and national, its idealizations are those we can identify with the values held by a community at large and it has the potential to mediate between popular and academic interest (p. 6). Like the men from Snipe Lake during the "war to end all wars," *Dancing in Poppies* has a contribution to make which is both culturally particular and culturally broad, and its reception in Canada outside of its birthplace will be one measure of the extent to which the collective national identity has come to embrace regional difference.

The Writers

GAIL BOWEN is perhaps best known as a novelist whose detective series featuring Joanne Kilbourn now includes eight books: *Deadly Appearances* (1990), *Murder at the Mendel* (1991), *The Wandering Soul Murders* (1992), *A Colder Kind of Death* (winner of the Crime Writers of Canada Arthur Ellis Award, 1994), *A Killing Spring* (1996), *Verdict in Blood* (1998), *Burying Ariel* (2000) and *The Glass Coffin* (2002). Her novels situate the puzzles of detective fiction within the context of everyday domestic life and work in a Prairie city and have been so popular that the first six have already aired as made-for-television movies.

What is less well known is that Bowen's writing career actually began in the 1980s and that she has also developed a string of successful stage plays simultaneously with her detective series. In response to an invitation by Ron Marken, the editor of the satirical *Easterners' Guide to Western Canada* (1985), Bowen (under the name of Hildy Rhodes) created a letter from a transplanted private school girl from the East describing a western form of entertainment—the belly-bumping contest. Hildy inspired publisher Rob Sanders to suggest that Marken and Bowen collaborate on more letters from these East-West perspectives which resulted in the novella, *1919: The Love Letters of George and Adelaide* (1987). When this book came to the attention of Susan Ferley, Artistic Director of the Globe Theatre in Regina, it led to the commissioned stage adaptation which came to be known as *Dancing in Poppies* (1993). Subsequent Globe Theatre premieres of Bowen's work included an adaptation of *Beauty and the Beast* (Christmas, 1993), *The Tree* (Christmas, 1994), and an adaptation of *Peter Pan* (Christmas, 1997). *Peter Pan* was produced by the Manitoba Theatre for Young People (Christmas, 2000) and this led to the commission of Bowen's most recent play, *Winnie and Co.*, which will premiere at MTYP in December of 2003. Bowen has a special affinity for adaptations. She enjoys "taking old stories and making them fresh for young people."

Although Bowen's writing career began at the age of 43 much of her writing draws upon earlier life experience. For instance, she has remarked that war, which was the catalyst for *Dancing in Poppies*, has defined much of her life. Born Gail Bartholomew, she grew up in Toronto in a house built by her grandfather, who fought in World War I and was killed on Armistice Day (after the armistice was signed). She recalls her grandmother and her friends, most of whom were war widows, talking about experiences similar to those that Adelaide recounts. When his daughter was born in 1942, Bowen's father was a sergeant and away for the first five years of her life. She remembers his war stories and that many of his friends were killed in the war. She also remembers an uncle who was traumatized by the death of a brother to the point of abandoning his wife and children for three years. Within her own family, then, Bowen saw how war—including World War I—changed things and remolded Canada. It would have been unimaginable to her grandmother that she would one day have dinner with a prince—and equally unimaginable that she would take a draft dodger as her husband.

Given this background, it is perhaps not surprising that she reports feeling "a connection with this play more than any of her other writing," but war is not the only point of connection between the writer and her writing. Like Roger, Bowen developed an early love for reading, writing and literature. She apparently "learned to read by the age of 3 from tombstones in Prospect Cemetery." Her love of reading developed further when she contracted polio at age 5, and she demonstrated prophetically early interest in writing for royalty when at the age of 10 she penned a letter to the Queen on the occasion of her coronation. While waiting for a royal response to her writing—which did not come until Prince Edward's visit to the Globe in 1994—she pursued her interest in literature at the University of Toronto (BA), the University of Waterloo (MA) and the University of Saskatchewan where she completed all but the dissertation component of the PhD. She taught extension courses in small town Saskatchewan and eventually joined the faculty at the Saskatchewan Indian Federated College (affiliated with the University of Regina) where she is currently Associate Professor and Head of the Department of English. She is married to Ted Bowen and has 3 children (Hildy, 30; Max, 28; and Nat, 22) and two grandchildren.

Like Bowen, **RON MARKEN** is a professor of English and university administrator. Formerly Head of the Department of English at the University of Saskatchewan (1991–95), he is currently Director of the

Gwenna Moss Teaching and Learning Centre. While Bowen's roots are in the East, Marken's roots are firmly planted in the West. He was born in Camrose, Alberta and studied at Concordia College, Moorhead, Minnesota (BA Hons 1960) and the University of Alberta (MA 1968, PhD 1972). Having developed and presented live television satellite credit courses in 30 remote locations, he is a celebrated teacher. He has received both the University of Saskatchewan Master Teacher Award (1985) and the 3M National University Teaching Fellowship (1987) and has published articles and delivered over 30 lectures on the craft of teaching.

Roger's love of poetry and Jack, the Irish labour activist in Act II of *Dancing in Poppies*, owe much to Marken's research interests in modern Irish Literature, prosody and poetry. He is responsible for numerous scholarly articles, book chapters, reviews and conference papers on these and other topics, and he has edited the *Canadian Journal of Irish Studies*. He has been active on the Executive of the International Association for the Study of Anglo-Irish Literature and has served as President of the Canadian Association for Irish Studies (1997–99).

Marken is also much in demand as a consultant on effective writing and language to groups ranging from Corrections Canada to the Saskatchewan Power Corporation and is frequently interviewed by CBC. As a freelance journalist he has provided articles, reviews and photographs relating to Canadian theatre and poetry for magazines such as *Maclean's* and for CBC broadcast. He has edited not only *The Easterners' Guide to Western Canada* (1985) but also *Don't Steal This Book* (1975), a collection of prison poetry. His collaboration with Gail Bowen on *1919: The Love Letters of George and Adelaide* (1987) and *Dancing in Poppies* (1993) was preceded by other work as a creative writer which reflects his strong interest in both poetry and drama: two books of poetry, *Dark Honey* (1974) and *Cycles of Youth and Age* (1978), and four plays. An interest in historical material and/or adaptation are the common threads running throughout Marken's dramatic work. Three of his plays were produced by CBC radio: *Troll Tales*, a children's play based on three Norwegian folk tales; *Almost Like Being a Man*, a two-hander involving a local woman cast in a touring company's production of *A Doll's House* in 1905 Saskatoon; and *And I Haven't Had the Rheumatism Since*, a monologue based on the experiences of his Norwegian grandmother, Kari Haug Lewis. *Troll Tales* was later adapted as a stage play for performance by high school students, and Marken developed *And I Haven't Had the Rheumatism Since* into a stage play which premiered as *Flights of Angels* under the direction of Marina Endicott at Saskatoon's 25th Street Theatre in 1986. A powerful tribute to one of the many strong immigrant women who contributed to the character and fabric of western Canada, "*Flights of Angels* is braced with an obvious conflict between the extremes of Age and Youth, but the more subterranean stresses lie along the fault lines of Civilization and Wildness, Progress and Creativity, and Illusion and Belief. It's also a play about Language and Truth." Marken's current work as a creative writer involves an academic murder mystery. He is married to Patricia Mary Marken and has five children and eight grandchildren.

Mary Blackstone,
Department of Theatre
University of Regina
July 2002

Works Cited

Unless otherwise noted all quotations from Gail Bowen, Susan Ferley and Ron Marken are from the unpublished interviews cited below. Gail Bowen's papers relating to the development of her fiction and drama are housed in the University Archives, University of Regina. Ron Marken's papers, including the texts of his unpublished plays, as well as 25th Street Theatre's archives, are housed in the University Archives, University of Saskatchewan. Archives for the Globe Theatre during Susan Ferley's tenure as Artistic Director are housed in the Saskatchewan Archives Board, but they are currently uncatalogued and normally unavailable to the public. Thanks are due to the Globe Theatre and, in particular, Susan Parkin for seeing that these archives were made available. Thanks are also due to the Globe Theatre and the Saskatchewan Archives Board for permission to cite from the archival materials and reproduce the photos contained in this edition.

Altman, Rick. "A Semantic/Syntactic Approach to Film Genre." *Cinema Journal* 23, no. 3 (1984): 6–18.
Bell, Lynne. "Canadian Powwow." *Majesty* 15, no. 10: 22–24.
Bowen, Gail. *Burying Ariel*. Toronto: McClelland & Stewart, 2000.
——. *A Colder Kind of Death*. Toronto: McClelland & Stewart, 1994.
——. *Deadly Appearances*. Vancouver: Douglas & McIntyre, 1990.
——. Interview with Mary Blackstone. Regina, Saskatchewan. April 2002.
——. *A Killing Spring*. Toronto: McClelland & Stewart, 1996.
——. *Murder at the Mendel*. Toronto: McClelland & Stewart, 1991.
——. *Pale Criminal*, forthcoming 2002.
——. *Verdict in Blood*. Toronto: McClelland & Stewart, 1998.
——. *The Wandering Soul Murders*. Vancouver: Douglas & McIntyre, 1992.

Bowen, Gail and Ron Marken. *1919, The Love Letters of George & Adelaide*. Saskatoon: Western Producer Prairie Books, 1987.

Davitt, Patrick. "Upfront." *Leader-Post,* August 8, 1994, C3.

Ferley, Susan. Telephone interview with Mary Blackstone. London, ON/Regina, SK. May 2002.

Knowles, Ric. *The Theatre of Form and the Production of Meaning: Contemporary Canadian Dramaturgies*. Toronto: ECW Press, 1999.

Kugler, D.D. Interview with Judith Rudakoff as published in *Between the Lines: The Process of Dramaturgy*. Eds. Judith Rudakoff and Lynn M. Thomson. Toronto: Playwrights Canada, 2002; pp. 93–112.

Lecker, Robert. "A Country Without a Canon?: Canadian Literature and the Esthetics of Idealism." *Mosaic* 26, no. 3 (Summer 1993): 1–19.

Lynde, Denyse. "In/Visible Drama of Atlantic Canada," in *Contemporary Issues in Canadian Drama*. Ed. Per Brask. Winnipeg: Blizzard, 1995; pp. 235–47.

Marken, Ron. *Cycles of Youth & Age*. Chipping Norton: Wychwood Press, 1978

——. *Dark Honey*. Saskatoon: Thistledown Press, 1976.

——, ed. *Don't Steal This Book*. Toronto: Green Tree Publishing, 1974.

——, ed. *The Easterners' Guide to Western Canada*. Saskatoon: Western Producer Prairie Books, 1985.

——. Interview with Mary Blackstone. Regina, SK. March 2002.

O'Connor, Kevin. "Prince's Regina Stay Ends: Was a Model of How Working Visits Should Go." *Leader-Post*, August 17, 1994.

Pilon, Bernard. "A Canadian War Story: 'Dancing in Poppies' Looks for Love after Horror." *Leader-Post*, February 15, 1993, C4. A3.

——. "Globe Gets Royal Patron." *Leader-Post*, March 12, 1992. A1.

——. "A Wake-up Call about the Power of Change." *Leader-Post*, February 19, 1993. C10.

——. "A Whole New Way to Write: Adapting Novella a Challenge for Regina Writer Gail Bowen." *Leader-Post*, February 15, 1993, C5.

Sutter, Trevor. "Prince Tastes Native Culture." *Leader-Post*, August 15, 1994, A3.

——. "Prince's Visit a Treat." *Leader-Post*, August 15, 1994. A1.

Winters, Bill. "Royalty Comes to Scarth Street." *Uptown* 3, no. 8 (August 1994): 7–9.

Selected Dates

June 28, 1914	Assassination of the Archduke Franz Ferdinand of Austria
July 28, 1914	Austria declares war on Serbia
August 4, 1914	Great Britain declares war on Germany
August 23, 1914	Battle of Mons
April–May 1915	Battle of Ypres
January 28, 1916	Women granted the vote in Manitoba
March 14, 1916	Women granted the vote in Saskatchewan
July–November 1916	Battle of the Somme
April 9–12, 1917	Battle of Vimy Ridge
April 12, 1917	Women granted the vote in Ontario
October 26– November 10, 1917	Battle of Passchendaele
December 6, 1917	The Halifax explosion
May 1918	Women granted the vote in Canadian federal elections
November 11, 1918	Armistice
May 15–June 21, 1919	Winnipeg General Strike
August 11– October, 1919	HRH The Prince of Wales Canadian Tour

Dancing in Poppies was first produced at the Globe Theatre, Regina, Saskatchewan in February of 1993 with the following cast and production team:

Adelaide Farlinger (18 years old)	Burgandy Code
Roger Currie (25 years old)	Mike Stack
George McTaggart (23 years old)	Tom Rooney

Director	Susan Ferley
Dramaturg	Mary Blackstone
Set and Lighting Designer	John Thompson
Costume Designer	Russell Danielson
Sound Designers	Rob Bryanton and Jim Folk
Choreographer	Christine Trapp
Stage Manager	Teresa Hiorns
Assistant Stage Manager	Lisa Roy
Apprentice Stage Manager	Dani Phillipson

The play and production were subsequently adapted for a one-hour performance on the occasion of the visit of His Royal Highness The Prince Edward, patron of the Globe Theatre, on August 14, 1994. The production was also adapted to tour to 20 towns and cities in Saskatchewan in October and November of 1994 with the following changes in cast and crew:

Roger Currie	Marcel Jeannin
Stage Manager	Michelle Cook

The play will receive its next production in October of 2002 at the Grand Theatre in London, Ontario.

ACT ONE

PHOTO BY LAURENT ROY, SOHO PHOTOGRAPHY
PHOTO COURTESY OF GLOBE THEATRE AND THE SASKATCHEWAN ARCHIVES BOARD

Scene 1

Lights out (totally black)

Darkness persists until audience grows quiet. We hear a harmonica playing "The World is Waiting for the Sunrise."

Then, from the darkness…

ROGER/OUT *(to the audience)*   Nothing has a beginning.

There is no first moment. You can point to no solitary word, no shaft of light across the path and say, "There … that's where it started."

Threads can be traced. They can be followed back into earlier stories. You will always find scraps and tissues of former reports. Within every tale that begins "Once upon a time," there is an infinite number of stories, each with its own "Once" and its own "time."

So … where we begin is arbitrary, perhaps even whimsical. We go to a play.

Someone turns out the lights. We sit a moment in the dark. The lights come on. And we're off. That's the convention, isn't it?

Mike Stack as Roger Currie

But our play starts a bit differently: Tonight we begin in the dark. It's no accident. Our play is about darkness... About how easy it is to take wrong paths, to get lost, to give way to fear, to believe that, for the rest of our lives, there will be nothing but darkness.

Our play is also about light.

The flare of a match.

It's a miracle, isn't it — how all the darkness in the theatre can't swallow this one small light, how this tiny light can transform the darkness?

Roger uses his match to light a lantern. He peers out into the theatre.

You're an attractive group, and you showed up here tonight, which suggests you're clever. The sort who would be good companions. Come with me...

Cast your eye back — as they used to say to us in school — "cast your eye back to another time."

Are you ready?

1918.

Trains burned coal. Schoolchildren learned Latin. Collars were high and hot. There were wooden plank sidewalks where you could lose your jackknife forever between the cracks. Cars were few and noisy. Dresses were long. Jaw-breakers were one cent for a bag full.

Roger tips his outrageous, checked hat mockingly.

ROGER   By the way, I'm Roger Currie. How do you do?

We were having a war then. The Great War. The War to End All Wars — that's what the politicians and the generals called it. And who among us has ever known a politician or a general to lie?

I, for one, enlisted because I wanted to make the world safe for democracy. Or maybe because tipping over outhouses at Hallowe'en no longer answered my need for excitement. Doesn't matter. It's all water under the privy now. All that counts is that I enlisted. And so did George here. You're going to like George. He's one of those farm boys who makes Canada famous: strong, loyal, hard-working.

George enters singing "Over There"

ROGER/OUT   Well, for some of us — like me and Enrico Caruso here — it was over over there sooner than we expected.

When we were invalided back to Canada, George with a limp and I — well — I had no eyes. So when they sent us to St. Andrew's Hospital in Toronto — St. Andrew himself probably died in it! — I couldn't see what a rat hole it really was. But I had other ways of knowing. I had my sources.

Adelaide enters

St. A's is *one* of the places where our play begins. On our last day at the convalescent hospital.

GEORGE   I'll bet the day we left Saskatoon station was one of the most exciting days in Canadian history … Addy, it was like we were royalty. People cheering and the band from the Collegiate played every tune they knew at least three times over.

Roger plays something stirring on his harmonica. Throughout his scenes, Roger's harmonica acts as a kind of musical reflection of his thoughts and feelings.

They couldn't get enough of us. Mothers, fathers, sweethearts, friends. There was such a crowd around the train I thought we were never going to get to the War. Someone gave me a bunch of flowers.

ROGER   Don't get too excited, George. They were only marigolds.

GEORGE   I leaned out of the train and lifted a young woman right off the ground. I kissed her, smack on the lips and carried her along for fifty yards. She held on as if I was the Prince of Wales.

ROGER   You wouldn't let her go! She was kicking like a fish on a line!

GEORGE   She enjoyed it — It was the least she could do for a hero in the making.

And now — "The Blind and Halt Platoon from Saskatoon" is heading home again. Victorious!

What a squad, eh Roger? Look at us!

ROGER   We're like something from one of those books my Aunt Edna used to give me to help me build my character:

"Once upon a time, there were two men. One was blind and one was lame, but They Refused To Let Their Infirmities Get

The Better Of Them. Because he could walk, the blind man carried the lame man upon his shoulders.

Because he could see, the lame man guided and counselled the blind man.

Boys and girls, when Adversity visits, just remember those two plucky fellows…"

GEORGE   My Aunt always gave me long underwear.

ROGER   Probably more useful, George, when the cold wind blows. But let's give Aunt Edna the benefit of the doubt and see where her story takes us. Turn the tale upside down. Get down on your knees. You can carry me. I'll be the guide!

ADELAIDE   You're going to have to rely on your own two feet, Roger. It'll be months before George is strong enough to carry you. But you'll be able to do your part. You'll make a wonderful guide.

GEORGE   None better! The men in our unit used to say that the army could drop Roger Currie anywhere in France or Belgium and within fifteen minutes, he'd find beer.

ROGER   Ignore him, Addy. He's always envied me my talents. A guide? Once, perhaps. Now you are my guide. I can't even find the dining hall on my own.

Come over here and sit beside me. Have a look out the window and tell me what the common folk are doing today.

ADELAIDE   I can see two boys, about twelve — old enough to be in school, come to think of it; but who could blame boys for playing hookey on an afternoon like this? Oh Roger, it is such a perfect fall day. The sidewalks are covered with leaves, coppery-red and yellow and orange. It's as if someone has spread out a magnificent Persian carpet to carry us over the city.

ROGER   The air smells of bonfires. Dead leaves. The beginning of winter … that's my favorite scent you're wearing, Addy.

ADELAIDE   It's called *Nuit de joie*. It's from Paris.

ROGER *(aside)*   I've been to France. It doesn't smell like that.

Were you ever in Paris, Addy?

ADELAIDE   Only in my dreams. I'm a world traveler in my dreams…

O look, our friend the pushcart man just came round the corner. He's making popcorn and he has a little stove to keep the butter hot. The boys have made themselves conkers…

GEORGE   What're they?

ROGER   Chestnuts drilled through the middle and then fastened on a string.

ADELAIDE   Don't you make conkers in Saskatchewan?

ROGER   We saw them in Hyde Park, remember?

ADELAIDE   You do have chestnuts there, don't you?

GEORGE   Chestnuts? In Snipe Lake, we don't even have trees! You can see Rosetown from our farm ... and that's fifty miles away!

ROGER   You dream you're in Paris. In my dreams, I'm in the Rockies, Addy. I climb to the peak of the tallest mountain and when I look around, I can see ... I can see everything.

Adelaide reaches out and touches his hand. Long Pause.

ADELAIDE   The boys are having a wonderful time. Conker to conker combat. If the papers are right, it won't be long before the only combat *will* be boys playing at war. *The Independent* says we're going to have an armistice before Christmas. Wouldn't peace be a shining star for all our trees?

ROGER/OUT *(turns from the scene, addresses the audience)*   She's perfect, isn't she? How she got that way is a mystery. Her father is a Bay Street Baron. She has a chauffeur and a cook and maids. She's an only child. She should be spoiled rotten, but nothing could spoil Adelaide Farlinger. Not even St. Andrew's Convalescent Hospital, and that place was the ruin of many a good woman.

Do you know what ruined those sweet-smelling idealistic girls? Misery. There was no way to inoculate them against what they saw when they looked at us. We were the boys who should have been writing them sonnets or whirling them around the dance floor. But we were broken men — eyesores, so those sweet-smelling girls closed their eyes and their ears and their minds and began to chirp [*in falsetto*]: "And how are we today? A little down in the dumps — lost your best friend? Oh you did. And your faith in your fellow man? Really. And in God. Now I don't like the sound of that. Well, I'll bring you a nice cup of cocoa — and if you'll turn that frown upside down, I might even bring a biscuit.

Adelaide was never like that. She knew some things were beyond the reach of a nice cozy cup of cocoa. She knew how to listen and she knew how to be silent. And that was a lifeline for us. We needed to know there was one other human being who understood that we were scared and angry and confused. Adelaide made us believe that, despite mountains of evidence to the contrary, there was reason to hope. And that was a rare and precious gift.

GEORGE *(reading)*   It says, "Railway Strike Imminent." Oh, and listen to this…

"City Workers Vote to Strike: 2,000 City of Toronto workers voted yesterday to strike for higher wages. This will consist of all outdoor workers, including septic tank employees!"

ROGER   Relax, McTaggart. The men of City Council will leap into the breach. They're used to shovelling…

GEORGE   Roger!

ADELAIDE   George, what do you think about all that talk of peace in *The Independent*?

GEORGE   Not much, Adelaide. It's just the usual rumours.

ROGER   We've had that optimistic claptrap ever since we started the killing. "We'll have the lads home by Christmas. Don't you worry."

Throughout the next few exchanges, Adelaide pays rapt attention, especially to Roger. She is, as she says later, "learning."

GEORGE *(scanning the paper)*   Well, according to the paper, there are a lot of lads who won't be home for Christmas:

"London: British casualties during the month of June totalled 141,147. This compares favourably with the total of 166, 802 reported during May…"

ROGER *(interrupting)*   "Favourably?" "Favourably!!"

That's 5,000 men a day! Four casualties a minute!!

GEORGE   Perhaps that's why there are still men ready to do their duty. It says here in *The Globe* that "… because they are anxious to get overseas, 20 mechanics of the Royal Air Force were discharged today into the Canadian army, with which they will go overseas immediately."

ROGER   At the current rate, they'll last five minutes — four casualties a minute! They should stand those newspaper owners on the front, arm them with their own propaganda and send them in! … "Anxious to get overseas" — bastards!

GEORGE   Still, you have to admire those mechanics. They're heroes in my book.

ROGER   Ah, *McTaggart's Book of Heroes* — not many words, but lots of nice pictures of flags and happy Canadian soldiers doing their part.

GEORGE There's nothing wrong with being proud of doing your part, Roger.

Now, Addy, here's an answer to your question about when the war will end. Straight from the horse's mouth — a general giving a speech in Montreal says, "This war will end when somebody's licked. We are not going to be licked. The army does not know when the war will end, and the army does not care. When the army has won, the war will end."

Laughing. That's army talk, Addy. Clear as mud.

ROGER Of course, McTaggart, it *is* a shame to end the war. Remember that piece out of the *Times*?

"Send the troops plenty of peppermints. The open-air life, the regular and plenteous feeding, …" What's that next bit?

GEORGE "… the exercise, and the freedom from care and responsibility…"

ROGER Right, how could I forget "the freedom from care and responsibility"?

GEORGE & ROGER *(in unison)* "Keep the soldiers extraordinarily fit and contented."

ADELAIDE Why would they say that when they know it's a lie?

ROGER Just gas from a talking blimp — Lord Northcliffe of the House of Lords. If all the fat cats who'd lied about the war were laid end to end, there wouldn't be a trollop from here to Picadilly Circus with a moment free.

Adelaide laughs

ROGER I'm sorry, Addy, that's rough talk in front of a lady.

ADELAIDE Not a lady, a young woman completing her education… You've taught me so much Roger. But I'm just beginning.

Clock chimes. Long pause.

ROGER Time, Gentlemen.

GEORGE *(to Adelaide)* That's what Molly, the barmaid at the World's End used to say at closing time. It meant we could have one more round…

ROGER Then it was out of the warmth and back into the cold cruel world…

GEORGE   Except for Joe Messenger. He could always coax Molly into one last drink and one last fumble in the back room. Come on, Roger, let's go say goodbye to him.

ROGER   No.

GEORGE   What do you mean 'No'? He's our friend. We were together all the time over there. The least we can do is…

ROGER   The least we can do is what, McTaggart? Say goodbye? We already have. We said goodbye to the Joe Messenger we knew at the Somme. That pathetic creature in there isn't Joe. It would be a waste of time.

GEORGE   You saved his life, Roger.

ROGER   And you saved mine. Take a good look McTaggart. What do you think? Was it worth it?

GEORGE   I don't ask myself questions like that, Roger. They're a waste of time.

George leaves. Adelaide moves closer to Roger.

ADELAIDE   Why is it that it's only when a friend is leaving that a person thinks of all the things she should have said? All the questions she should have asked?

ROGER   What questions should you have asked me, Addy?

ADELAIDE   *Pause.* What you wanted more than anything in life… Roger, what would you ask for if, right now, a genie appeared and said he'd grant you one wish?

ROGER   I'd ask…

No that would be too much to ask.

I think I'd tell that genie I wanted to see the Rockies. With you, Addy. In the springtime when the fields are alive with wildflowers and the mountain peaks are covered with snow and the sky is the colour of a robin's egg.

My Mother and Dad had a calendar like that years ago. Where we live is pretty flat country and those mountains on the calendar were magic to me. I thought they went straight to God.

Pause.   What would you ask the genie for, Addy?

ADELAIDE   That your wish came true. That all your wishes come true … Oh Roger, I don't know how to say goodbye.

ROGER   Then I'll teach you. I can do that for you, at least. It never gets easy, but it's better if you keep it simple… Goodbye, Addy.

PHOTO BY LAURENT ROY, SOHO PHOTOGRAPHY
PHOTO COURTESY OF GLOBE THEATRE AND THE SASKATCHEWAN ARCHIVES BOARD

Left to right: Mike Stack as Roger Currie, Tom Roonie as George McTaggart, Burgandy Code as Adelaide Farlinger

She moves closer to him. The sexual tension between them is almost palpable. Finally Adelaide reaches her hand towards Roger's cheek. At that moment George re-enters. He is wearing his army cap and jacket, ready to travel.

GEORGE   I gave Joe your regrets, Roger.

Here's your kit bag. We have to be at Union Station by four.

Adelaide, I'll really miss you. Promise if you're out our way, you'll stop by. You'd love Saskatchewan. It's the best place on earth.

ADELAIDE   I promise.

To both of them but really to Roger.

This time next week you'll be fifteen hundred miles away from me. I looked Saskatoon up in the Atlas. I hadn't realized our country was so big. When I was little, Toronto seemed like all the world any of us would ever have to know. The war has changed so many things.

ROGER   The war has changed everything, Addy.

Picks up his checked cap.

Time's up. What do you think of my hat?

ADELAIDE   It certainly makes an impression.

ROGER   I got it from a man at Union Station.

"Hey! Over here! You! Soldier boy. Yes, you. Time to toss the tin-pot hat and get into something more lively. Just...

Step right up. I've got derbies, bowlers, Stetsons, bicornes,

Tam-o-shanters, toques, fedoras, tricornes.

I've got panamas, pith helmets, deerstalkers too,

Sou-westers, sombreros — hey — a top hat would look good on you

Two dollars. But for you, I'll sacrifice it for a singleton. Because you served your country. Whaddya say?

Pause   Good choice — bold, but not loud. A hat for a man who stands out in a crowd."

Do you really like it, Addy?

ADELAIDE   It's perfect — one of a kind, just like you. I'll be able to spot that cap anywhere in Canada. Besides, I know where to find you. Remember, Saskatchewan is in my Atlas. You're going to a better land,

Speaking, then gradually into poetry, then song…

> Where everything is bright
> Where handouts grow on bushes
> And you sleep out every night

Roger, then George, joining her singing…

> Where you don't have to work at all
> Or even change your socks,
> And little streams of whiskey
> Come trickling down the rocks.

Scene 2

Fade up on George and Roger on the farm in Snipe Lake

GEORGE   C'mon, you can help me with the milking. Just try it. It's easy. You don't have to see what you're doing — it's all in the fingers.

ROGER   Milking? Don't you remember? You did that yesterday. No one could drink that much milk.

GEORGE *(laughing)*   Stop it, Roger! Those cows will explode if we don't milk them!

ROGER   Do you mean you have to go out there and pull on those udder things every day? That's very odd! You didn't mention milking when you enumerated the charms of country living. I saw myself more as a squire of the manor.

GEORGE *(laughing)*   And me as the hired man who does the work... No, Roger, I'm afraid on a farm everybody works — even an old army chum who's been invited out to cure his nerves.

ROGER *(suddenly very agitated)*   There's nothing wrong with my nerves, McTaggart. They are responding appropriately to circumstances. The man who's really in need of a nerve-cure is the one who sees what we saw over there and comes back and picks up where he left off, no questions asked.

Recites   I knew a simple soldier boy
            Who grinned at life in empty joy,
            Slept soundly through the lonesome dark,
            And whistled early with the lark.
            In winter ... in winter...

What's the rest of the line? I used to know this. The words are all I have now, George. I can't lose them.

GEORGE   It's all right. Everything's going to be all right. Just let me get the book.

George moves to the sideboard and picks up a book. It's apparent from his actions that this scene has been played out between the two men many times. George reads:

– 13 –

> In winter trenches, cowed and glum,
> With crumps and lice and lack of rum,
> He put a bullet through his brain.
> No one spoke of him again.[1]

GEORGE   Roger! I don't mind reading to you, but does it have to be this depressing stuff? It just makes you feel worse. Why can't you choose something more … more … inspirational?

ROGER   Inspirational? How about a little Kipling? Bloodyard Kipling, the prophet of jingoism? My God! You might as well be reading Mother Goose! "All the king's horses and all the king's men couldn't put Humpty together again." *Listen* to what you just *said*!

With intensity

"Sneak home and pray you'll never know / The hell where youth and laughter go." Sent to hell by lies and duplicity. They don't know, George. They'll never know, will they? Never.

GEORGE   At ease, Roger. That's behind us now. It's over.

George lights the lantern and hands it to Roger.

C'mon. The least you can do is carry the lantern.

ROGER   Ah — a Canadian Diogenes, wandering around, looking for an honest man and never finding him.

GEORGE   Actually, I was just thinking you might light my way to the barn. But if that doesn't appeal to you, I'll give you a sack of feed and you can throw it to the chickens.

ROGER   Like a politician spreading his promises. I'd like that. Just don't let them foul my clothing.

GEORGE *(laughing)*   Fine! I'll stand you on a chair above your electorate, and you can cast forth your bounty.

ROGER   It will be like our chaps in the artillery, won't it? Let the shells fall where they may! Chickens beware!…

Pause   … and find my gas mask. Do you have any idea how much this farm *stinks*, McTaggart?

GEORGE   It's the smell of life and food in the making, Roger — before it's all washed and neatly wrapped for you city folk.

ROGER   I'll never eat again.

---

1. Siegfried Sassoon, "Suicide in the Trenches," *Counter-Attack and Other Poems*. 1918

GEORGE   Well, that's good news! Since you arrived last Friday, you've nearly cleaned me out!

ROGER   What a miserable day, that was. Riding with that Raleigh man in the rain. Almost made me homesick for the trenches! I thought we'd be bumping into the ark any second!

GEORGE   But you shouldn't have kidded him like that! He was good enough to bring you all the way out here from the station.

ROGER   But why, McTaggart — why — why would a man with a lisp work for the Raleigh company? "Waleigh man! Waleigh! Anyone need Waleigh pwoducts?" And I didn't kid him. All I did was ask, "Why don't you work for Watkins!" It was an innocent observation about the absurdity of human existence.

GEORGE   I guess you have to be from a big place like Saskatoon to see the absurdity of human existence.

ROGER   Addy would get the point of that story. She always got the point of my stories. She knew how to listen… And she knew how to laugh.

Roger falls silent, remembering.

We hear dance music. Lights up on Addy laughing. George is in her arms, trying to escape.

GEORGE   I know the doctors say dancing is good for my leg, but there must be some exercise I could do that would be easier on you. Your poor feet.

ADELAIDE   My feet are fine. I come from stout Farlinger stock. It'll take more than a few little bumps to do me in. Now come on. One more waltz and you're free.

GEORGE   No, Addy, this sod buster is hanging up his dance shoes. Go get Roger. He could use a few social graces.

The music changes to "The World Is Waiting For The Sunrise." Adelaide goes to Roger and takes his hand in hers.

ADELAIDE   May I have this dance?

Roger goes to her wordlessly, and they dance, very seriously and quite well. It's apparent that they are enjoying the chance to be in one another's arms. Then Roger dances Adelaide too close to the doorframe. As her arm hits the doorframe Addy cries out in pain, and Roger becomes savage. His anger is directed first at the doorframe. Then as the music continues, saccharine and irrelevant, he hits out at the Victrola which screeches, then growls to a stop. Adelaide goes to him, soothing.

ADELAIDE   Roger, it's alright. It was nothing. It just startled me.

He turns from her. Adelaide pulls back her sleeve, takes Roger's hand and rubs it along the part of her arm that was injured.

ADELAIDE   There. Nothing's broken. Nothing's bruised.

ROGER   Your skin is so soft.

ADELAIDE   Shall we finish our dance?

ROGER   There's no music, Addy. I took care of that, too.

Adelaide takes his hand

ADELAIDE   We don't need the Victrola.

Adelaide begins to sing:

> Dear One, the world is waiting for the sunrise
> Every rose is heavy with dew
> The thrush on high
> His sleepy mate is calling
> And my heart is calling you.

ROGER   When I'm with you I can almost believe.

ADELAIDE   In what?

ROGER *(pause)*   Sunrises.

They dance again. They part and Roger moves back to the Snipe Lake scene.

ROGER   There's no dancing without her.

GEORGE   What?

ROGER   Nothing makes sense without her.

GEORGE   Well, she was the third point of our triangle.

ROGER   Not just the third point, George. She was the one at the top that gave the two of us a sense of direction.

GEORGE   We could write to her.

Roger seizes upon this.

ROGER   We'll tell her how everything's gone wrong since we left her. Then she'll know, George. We'll start with the welcome home we got from the good citizens of Saskatoon.

GEORGE   Roger, don't. It's over.

ROGER *(Ignoring him. Roger is already reliving the night they returned.)*
Take your blinkers off, McTaggart!

We were coming back from hell. A hundred thousand of our chums dead. It was hard not to envy them. At least they were out of it.

GEORGE   Then one day we were out of it too.

ROGER   They herded us into ships then they herded us onto trains. Finally, we came home … to silence. No bands. No cheers. Not even a politician. Just an empty train station.

GEORGE   Well, we didn't take it lying down.

ROGER   That was quite a night. Two men marching down Second Avenue at midnight singing

GEORGE   "It's a Long Way to Tipperary"!

ROGER   Everybody knew we were home then!

GEORGE   I guess we showed the world you can't ignore a couple of Canadian boys.

ROGER   The world *would* like to ignore us, though. Damn their simple souls! The Blind and Halt Platoon doesn't quite fit their romantic picture of a soldier boy.

GEORGE   But we were always good enough for Addy.

ROGER   We were that. George, get out your pen and paper. Let's let her know that the Platoon still needs her…

* * *

Lights up on Adelaide.

ADELAIDE   And I need the Platoon. When you were here, there was always something to look forward to: George's dancing lessons — remember Sod Buster's Ballroom? Or the three of us in the sunroom talking about what was in the papers or how the war was going. And Roger, remember how after lights out, you and I would just sit and be still together. I think I liked that best of all.

Now … *(Pause.)* Joe Messenger is slipping farther from me everyday. I have nightmares where he grows smaller and smaller, and I wake up with my heart pounding, terrified that he's going to disappear altogether. My father says the sleepless nights are ruining my looks and that the work at St. A's is coarsening me. He wants me to quit. He says it's time for me to stop associating with soldiers and meet some nice young men. I can't believe my own father would say something so stupid and cruel. But at least his cruelty is out there in the open. The polite ones who look through the men are worse. Most of the "bad cases," like Oliver, don't want to be taken out on walks any more. They'd rather stay in this gloomy old building than watch people turn their eyes away when they walk by.

Yesterday I took Oliver down to get some popcorn from the man on the corner. It was his prize for beating me at euchre. He was so proud of himself. Then a woman walked by with her little boy. Do you know what she said? "Don't stare at the poor man. You'll hurt his feelings."

Well, Oliver will get through this. If he could go on living after half of his body had been seared by a flamethrower, I guess he can endure a stupid woman.

One thing is certain: he won't have to endure it without me. I'm here for as long as Joe and Oliver and the others want me, and my father is just going to have to get used to it.

Fade down on Adelaide.

PHOTO BY LAURENT ROY, SOHO PHOTOGRAPHY
PHOTO COURTESY OF GLOBE THEATRE AND THE SASKATCHEWAN ARCHIVES BOARD

Mike Stack as Roger Currie

Left to right: Tom Roonie as George McTaggart, Mike Stack as Roger Currie,
Background: Burgandy Code as Adelaide Farlinger

Left to right: Mike Stack as Roger/Jack, Tom Roonie as George

Burgandy Code as Adelaide Farlinger

Scene 3

This scene should be done like a trio — in music and dance — moving quickly from one character to another as each gives her/his account of the Armistice — George & Roger in Saskatoon, Adelaide in Toronto. These juxtaposed impressions should create a mood that moves from excitement and happiness to something more menacing and out of control (paralleled by Roger's drinking). The scene should end with the sense that elation, too soon, gives way to depression — to the hangover after the party. Throughout the scene there are bursts of music from Roger's harmonica.

GEORGE There is no darkness in Saskatoon. That's what I'll remember about November 11th, 1918!

ADELAIDE It's over! The grandfather clock in our front parlour just struck three.

GEORGE The sky is *filled* with *light*! Light! Light from the bonfires in the streets. Light from burning haystacks in the countryside. And Northern Lights … the whole sky is glowing! The heavens are dancing for peace!

You'd love it Adelaide!

ROGER The bottles are uncorked.

ADELAIDE All of Toronto looks different tonight. It looks as if it had heard the words "At Ease" tonight. Yes father, I'll be right there. Yes, it will be wonderful to see peace come to Bay Street.

ROGER Peace — that word! That sweet, *sweet* word.

GEORGE The whole city is a party! And we would have missed it all if Sliv Mitchell hadn't had to come to the city to pick up his false teeth. Well, God bless Sliv's choppers — I wouldn't have missed this night for anything. Girls in their Sunday best are dancing with men on crutches, old women are hiking up their skirts and dancing with one another. Mothers and Dads are laughing, crying… Boys are setting off firecrackers. Addy, there's so much going on. Train whistles! Bells ringing in all the steeples.

ROGER Liquor is flowing freely! Here's to you, Adelaide Farlinger.

ADELAIDE   Who could believe Toronto the Good could be so *bad*! I've been in my father's offices a hundred times, but I have never seen anything like this. Bay Street stockbrokers hurling ticker tape out of their office windows. It's amazing. They actually look as if they're having fun.

ROGER   We must be thankful that Saskatoon is temperance to the teeth. The Dear Lord alone knows what would happen if alcohol stripped the city's men of their inhibitions and released their baser selves!

ADELAIDE   Listen to that! Steam whistle blasts! I think they're coming from City Hall. If I just lean out the window a little more maybe I'll be able to see…

ROGER   I, like, the liquor, am flowing freely. I've been lost a dozen times. Each time I've been rescued by someone whose perfume smells better than the perfume of the one before. The woman I'm dancing with envelops me in violets. I'm sure she's as lovely as Helen of Troy.

GEORGE   More along the lines of the Trojan horse, but it doesn't matter. Tonight every woman is beautiful, and every man is brave.

ADELAIDE   They're dancing on Bay Street…

ROGER   Whiskey makes my lips too numb to harm on my humonica, so I must sing.

ROGER & GEORGE & ADELAIDE *(singing raucously)*:

> K-k-k-Katie! Beeyootifull Kateee
> Yer the only g-g-g-gurl
> That I ah-doooor!
> When the m-m-moon shines
> Over the cow-shed
> I'll be waiting at the k-k-k-kitchen dooor!

ADELAIDE   Mr. Pope, hello … Yes, a very happy day … I was so sorry to hear about Laurie … Passchendaele, wasn't it? … Yes, we were the same age — almost exactly. Yes, he was just a boy.

Of course, I'm old enough to drink a toast.

She lifts her glass

To the King. To Mr. Borden… and to Laurie.

GEORGE *(raising a bottle)*   To the girl in the photograph I saw my last day on the line. Her picture was in the hand of a dead man, a soldier lying face down in the mud of a shell hole. I think he was German, but somehow that doesn't matter anymore. He was a boy, and she was just a girl. That's what we should remember.

ROGER *(Very drunk. Lifts his bottle to the audience, a toasting gesture.)*

To the old men. The ones who have made such a botch of the first eighteen years of the century. Here's to them. Let's drink to them all. To the capitalists! To the politicians! To the ministers of God!! Let's drink to the fat, flatulent, greedy bunch of liars they have proven to be. Let's drink to them, and tonight when we kneel beside our little beds and say our "Now I lay me's" let's pray for the whole lot of them … to be blasted to hell!!

Roger passes out face down.

Scene 4

St. Andrew's Hospital

ADELAIDE *(writing)*   December 12, 1918. A month and a day after the armistice, but the mood at St. A's is black. The weather has been awful even for Toronto — I don't remember the last time I saw the sun. Every morning it's the same: snow, sleet, and the wind blowing off the lake —

But it isn't just the weather. It's everything. The end of the war has been so hard for the men. You know how they longed for peace, but they feel abandoned now that everyone else is moving ahead and they're left behind.

There's no change in Joe Messenger. I try to do what you did, George, sit with Joe and sing the songs you sang together in the old days at the World's End Pub. I don't sing them as well as you did, but he doesn't seem to mind.

I remember you saying how Joe loved to sing "When Irish Eyes Are Smiling" because it always made the girls come round.

I'd give anything to hear him sing. All he does is sit and look out the window. If you turn his chair so he faces the wall, he sits and looks at the wall. Windows or wall — it's the same to him.

I'm so afraid for him. And sometimes … I'm afraid for me.

* * *

In Snipe Lake…

ROGER   Damn it! That place is eating her alive, McTaggart. She should get out of there. She should save herself.

GEORGE   We don't always have choices, Roger. People have to help each other. You're a Canadian boy. You know that. And you know that even when the burden gets heavy, you don't just walk away… The chaps at St. A's need Adelaide, and she knows it.

ROGER   They *think* they need her. But they just *want* her.

Look at Messenger — he's past it. He doesn't need anything. It's all a waste...

GEORGE   He's still alive isn't he? Adelaide is one of the few good things that keeps Joe going. He'll pull out of it. He's got more courage than all of us put together. You must remember that.

ROGER   I remember that when those bastards sent us over the top, Joe Messenger always went first, like a bat out of hell. Yelling like a maniac. *(Pause.)* The last time, when I brought him back, he held onto me the way a child holds onto his mother. And he was crying. But it wasn't the way a kid cries. It was the sound an animal makes when it's caught in a trap.

Pause.

They always sent us over the top exactly at dawn. Did you ever think of the stupidity of it? First the artillery barrage. Then the barrage lets up, the cock crows, and we walk out to be shot. The other side could have set their watches by us.

Just once ... just *once* ... couldn't we have attacked them by surprise? At supper time, maybe? But that wouldn't have been "sporting" would it? Better to smash guys like Joe...

Roger is very worked up now

GEORGE   Roger. Roger. It's over. The fighting is over. Let's think about Addy. She needs us, Roger. Now. The third member of the Platoon... Let's write her.

ROGER *(he's not listening)*   Joe had eyes that made you want to laugh and be happy. At the "World's End" all he had to do was look at a girl and she'd throw herself at him. "You have lovely eyes," she'd say, and we knew she was a goner.

Roger plays "When Irish Eyes Are Smiling" on the harmonica.

* * *

ADELAIDE   He's dead. His eyes. They're the same. They were dead all along because he was dead all along. It was just his body hadn't caught up.

ROGER   Sweet Jesus, let it stop.

ADELAIDE   I found him. He was turning ever so gently in the wind. The floor was dusted with snow. He was wearing his uniform. Why would a soldier put on his uniform to end his life?

GEORGE   Why? I don't know, Addy. Maybe he didn't want

Left to right: Tom Roonie as George McTaggart, Mike Stack as Roger Currie,
Background: Burgandy Code as Adelaide Farlinger

to let the other boys down. The ones who were wearing their uniforms when they died over there. It doesn't make much sense does it. But none of this…

ADELAIDE   He was in the sunroom. He stood on a chair so he could tie the rope around his throat. Then he kicked the chair aside.

ROGER   Aaagh, Joe! All the King's horses and all the King's men couldn't put you together again. So you tied a rope around your neck, kicked over the chair and put an end to it. Put an end to the life I "saved."

GEORGE   Roger, don't. Just let him go.

ROGER   I need a drink. No, scratch that. I need a hundred drinks. I need, as we used to say in the old days, to get blind drunk. There's a bottle around here somewhere. Find it for me McTaggart. Remember "even when the burden gets heavy, a Canadian boy doesn't walk away."

George leaves and comes back with the bottle. He pours them each a drink. Roger tosses his back and pours himself another. Throughout the scene, Roger is drinking heavily.

GEORGE   Take it easy, Roger.

ROGER   "Take it easy Roger." Wake up, man. It's a wake. *(Laughs.)* It's Joe Messenger's wake and I'm the chief mourner. I have my rights. I'm the one who saved his life. If I'd left him on the battlefield he would have died. Died just like that. *(Snaps his fingers.)* But I didn't allow that to happen.

I tried to trick God. I tried to trick that kindly old white-bearded chap the chaplain used to tell us was always fighting right beside us in the trenches. God decided it was time for Joe Messenger to die, but I said 'no'.

I think I deserve a drink for that. A drink for the man who stood up to God and saved his chum's life. It was an act of courage above and beyond the call of duty. I have a medal to prove it.

Roger stumbles across the room, gets his medal and hands it to George.

Read the inscription McTaggart.

Pause.   Read the bloody inscription.

GEORGE   To Corporal Roger Allan Currie, for courage above and beyond the call of duty.

ROGER   Thank you. As Joe acknowledged when he put on his uniform that last time, it's good to know your government's behind you. Of course, saving Joe's life didn't work out the way it was supposed to. Instead of being restored to pink-cheeked good health, my friend spent six months in the land of the living dead before he got up "the courage above and beyond the call" to kill himself.

Pours another drink.   Alright, God, lesson learned. Whomever you have put asunder let no man try to join together. It's the lesson of Humpty Dumpty. Have you got that McTaggart? Sooner or later all of us, Joe, you, me, even our beautiful Addy. Sooner or later we will have to take the great fall. There's nothing we can do but be good little eggs and wait our turn.

GEORGE   I won't accept that.

ROGER   Won't accept what?

GEORGE   I won't accept that there's nothing we can do but wait to die. Life is what we make it. I may not have read the books you've read, Roger, but I know a few things. And one of the things I know is that you don't bring meaning to your life by bellyaching about how useless everything is. You bring meaning to your life by getting past your own skin and reaching out to the other fellow.

ROGER   Thank you Reverend McTaggart for that fine string of clichés.

GEORGE   What I say may sound old hat, but it's still true. People have to be able to count on each other. I'm just as broken up about Joe as you are. He was my friend too. But he's gone and there's someone alive who needs us. Listen to Addy's letter.

He reads

ADELAIDE   I'm so cold. The doctor says it's shock — because of finding Joe. He ordered me home to bed. I'm supposed to stay quiet and warm, but I can't get warm. No matter how many blankets I pile on top of me, I can't make the cold go away.

I don't know how much more I can take. I know the men at St. A's need me, but I don't want to be needed. I want out. I want to be young. I want to think about tea dances and the way my hair looks, God forgive me, I want to have a happy day — just one day where I don't have to see death and pain and loss.

I wish I could shut my eyes and make it all go away. I wish it could be the spring of 1912 before everything was ruined forever. I wish we could all be young again.

GEORGE   She needs help, Roger. What'll we do to help her?

ROGER   McTaggart, didn't you listen to what you read? No, you never do, do you? Addy says she wants one day where she doesn't have to see death and pain and loss. The last thing she needs is us. What have we got to offer a girl like Addy? The thing we should do is cut her loose. Give her her freedom. The way Joe Messenger did when he climbed up on that chair. Maybe we should follow his example.

Roger stands drunkenly.

Come on McTaggart, let's not wait to be pushed off that wall. Let's be heroes and leap.

George is silent.

Did you hear me?

GEORGE   Yes and I'm ignoring you. If you want to be an egg waiting to fall off a wall, go to it. It sounds pretty stupid to me, but I'm from Snipe Lake. We don't go in much for philosophy.

George leaves and comes back in with a piece of harness metal, sits again at the table and begins to work on it.

ROGER   What're you doing?

GEORGE   I'm making a present for Addy. Her birthday is coming up. New Year's Day, remember? She was born just as the bells were tolling in the twentieth century. I'm making her a medal to let her know she's the best thing about our new century and that in my opinion, as long as we have people like her who stick with people and don't give in, maybe we all have a chance.

Pause.   Go ahead and laugh if you want to. I know it sounds a bit thick.

ROGER *(Pause ... and then very quietly)*   Maybe when you're finished, I could help with the polishing.

GEORGE   I think that would work out fine. I always thought you had a lot of potential as a brass polisher.

* * *

ADELAIDE *(picks up the medal)*   Roger, do you remember telling me that you gave your medals from the Somme to a trollop in Picadilly Circus?

ROGER   Because she and I were fighting on the same side and we were both being diddled by generals!

ADELAIDE   All the trollops and all the generals in the world couldn't get me to part with my Snipe Lake medal. It's the most wonderful present I've ever been given. And I've done something to earn it!

I punched my Uncle William in the nose!

ROGER   The war goes on!

GEORGE *(reading)*   It happened on New Year's Eve.

ADELAIDE   All the Farlingers were at our house. They always gather here to see the New Year in. They were here the night I was born.

As usual, my Uncle William dominated the talk. He is deaf, and he is a fool. When he speaks, he removes his hearing apparatus. It's as if even he can't stomach the nonsense that comes out of his mouth.

GEORGE   On the night of December 31st, his topic was us — "The Younger Generation."

ROGER   Wait, let me guess what the old bugger said.

"All you young people live for is pleasure. You lack respect for God, the Monarchy, the Dominion and Your Elders etcetera.

You need a whipping. Spare the rod and spoil the children. Brats, the lot of them. We give the boys the adventure of war, and they come home and grouse about jobs. No spine. Convalescent hospitals full of them. 'Nerve cases,' they call themselves. Fakers, I call them. Rather lie about and be mollycoddled than go out and do a day's work. They're no better than the girls — pantywaists."

How did I do, McTaggart?

GEORGE *(laughing)*   Give or take a pantywaist or two — a hundred percent.

ADELAIDE   People sometimes say, "I saw red"? When Uncle William sat down, there were little red flecks in my vision. And then everything swam together.

You, Roger, who seem to slip further away from me every time you write. *(Long pause.)* George, with your strong body and wasted leg; Oliver with his handsome face melted by the flames; Joe Messenger who put on his uniform so we would know he died for his country.

"At St. Andrew's we despise old men like you who send young men off to war with lies about how sweet and glorious it is to die for their country. I'm ashamed of a country that would give her boys a parade when they went off to die, but couldn't find them a job when they came home to live. If you had any decency, Uncle William, you'd be ashamed too. The sight of your smug, lying face makes me sick."

Uncle William sprang out of his chair, and raised his hand to me. Then I raised mine.

The next moment he was sprawled on the floor with blood pouring out of his nose, ... and onto his dinner jacket. My knuckles were red with his blood, but I wasn't afraid. I looked him straight in the eye. 'That was a message from *our* generation.'

GEORGE   What a wonderful girl! Roger, do you see what can happen when people don't just sit back and let life happen to them? If we have the courage to stand up and be counted, we can defeat the Uncle Williams on every front.

ROGER   McTaggart, there must be something in the water here that preserves innocence. If I could come up with a way to bottle it, I could make a fortune. "Step right up, folks, and get a bottle of the famous Snipe Lake water — it cleans out your bowels and washes your mind free of rational thought."

There are tens of thousands of Uncle Williams out there. Dangerous powerful men. Addy can punch them all she likes, but they have the hammers. If she keeps on bloodying their noses, they'll get their revenge.

Pause.

But you're right about one thing, George. Adelaide Farlinger is a wonder!

* * *

ADELAIDE   For the first time in weeks I feel like me again, strong and happy. Punching Uncle William in the nose freed something in me, made me believe that we can make things right.

Even God seems to be on my side. This morning at Church, the reading was from Isaiah; the part where Isaiah says he is sent to comfort all those who mourn, "to give them garlands instead of ashes, oil of gladness instead of mourners' tears, a garment of splendour for the heavy heart."[2]

I've even bought my own garment of splendour — a new dress. And it's red. My first red dress. Roger, do you remember telling me that sometimes it's best not to make the sensible choice? Well Eaton's was full of sensible choices, but I didn't take any of them. "Gladness instead of tears" my new dress said, and that's what I longed for. Even the name of the material it's made of is magic. "Chiffon." Doesn't that sound like a kiss? And it feels like gossamer. This is a dress for dancing. When I turn, the red chiffon flows around me. I feel like I'm dancing in a field of poppies.

Throughout the following scene George's worry about Roger is apparent. Roger is silent and withdrawn, and George works hard to get some sort of response from him.

GEORGE (*putting down the letter*)   Can't you just see Adelaide in that red dress? I'll bet she's the prettiest girl in Toronto. Remember that time you asked me the colour of her hair?

Pause.

I said it was brown, and you got so mad at me. "Brown, brown, McTaggart. What kind of brown? Brown as a mud hen? Brown as a loaf of bread? Brown as a boot? Well, last night it came to me. Addy's hair is the colour of molasses taffy. When I was a kid, my mother used to make candy every Saturday. I could never wait for the taffy to cool, so she'd always pour a little bit on the snow for me. Did your mother ever do that?"

Pause.

Anyway, that's the colour of Addy's hair. The colour of molasses taffy on the snow — shiny brown with gold flecks. And that hair of hers has a mind of its own. It's always escaping from those pins girls use to put their hair up. Her eyes are dark, and they shine too.

Pause.

Would you like me to read to you? Some Siegfried Sassoon, if you like. Did I get the name right this time?

ROGER   You got it right, George.

---

2. Isaiah 61: 3.

GEORGE   Well, that's a first.

ROGER   No. You got a lot of things right, George. I don't think I've ever been very fair about that.

George picks up lantern.

I'm going to see to the animals Roger. There's a blizzard coming. It's forty below and I can smell the snow in the air. And listen to that wind. It's coming straight from the mountains. By morning we'll be snowed in. Anyway, I won't be too long. Keep yourself warm. After supper we'll sit by the stove and warm ourselves with thoughts of Addy.

George leaves.

ROGER   Addy. Lovely, lovely Addy. Tonight, for the first time, I can almost see you. A girl in a red dress, dancing in a field of poppies. Behind you a mountain soars so high its peak pierces the clouds. The sky is blue and when you lift your face to the sun, its warmth turns your cheeks to roses. I walk up behind you and touch the shoulder of your dress. You turn and reach your hand out to me. I take your hand in mine and then…

And then what? Where do I take you? There's nothing ahead but darkness.

Try to bring it back. A girl in a red dress, dancing in a field of poppies. Behind her a mountain. She lifts her face to the sun. I touch her shoulder… She turns… Sweet Jesus, it's not her face. It's his… . His eyes are looking straight into mine… He's just a kid. He's smiling at me… I can't kill him. But I have to. No choice… . I pull the pin and toss the grenade… It's going home. A perfect curve straight into his dugout. He's still smiling. I can't stop looking. Put your head down, Currie. But I can't. My eyes are locked into his… There's a flash and I see… I see his head lifting from his shoulders and arcing into the air… He's still smiling. The last face I will ever see.

Forgive me. Please forgive me. I'm sorry. They said we had to. I didn't have a choice.

He gives in to emotion. Then there is some sort of turning point for him, a moment of insight, and he is suddenly calm.

But I have a choice now. George said the wind was coming straight from the mountains. All I have to do is walk into the wind. As long as I can feel the wind in my face, I'll know I'm headed west. West to the Rockies. And when I can't walk any-

Mike Stack as Roger Currie, Burgandy Code as Adelaide Farlinger

more, I'll dig a little cave in the snow, and I'll crawl in and close my eyes and think of the girl in the red dress, and I won't stop thinking of her until the end comes and the snow covers us both.

Roger leaves. The sound of the blizzard, which has been building throughout the scene reaches its peak.

Against the blizzard sounds, we hear a harmonica playing a waltz. The harmonica grows fainter and fainter. Finally, there is silence.

George enters, begins calling Roger's name with increasing agitation as he realizes what has happened. At the last of the scene, he should shout Roger's name.

Then lights down.

Adelaide screams.

* * *

Lights up on the living room at Snipe Lake. George, obviously uncomfortable in a suit, enters. He stands for a moment, looking around as if he's never seen the room. In his hands is the memorial card from Roger's funeral. He looks at it and reads:

GEORGE   "Roger Allan Currie, born November 1, 1894, died, March 4, 1919." My mother used to tell me that March 4th was the only day of the year that gave a command.

Damn it, Roger, how could you do it? How could you just walk away?

That night you dragged Joe Messenger back ... the way he howled. I'd never heard a man in so much pain ... you held him in your arms and rocked him back and forth ... "It'll get better..." That's what you said to him ... Over and over that's what you said ... "Just hang on, and it'll get better."

Pause.

Did you believe what you told him, Roger? Did you believe what you said? Or were they just words? Just more of your bloody words...

Lights up on Adelaide

She is crying, but fighting it... She is wearing the red dress. In Act

I, Roger commented on her wonderful stillness; that stillness is gone now. She is wound very tight.

ADELAIDE   I'm going to spend my life making it up to you, Roger. I'll keep you alive in the hearts and minds of everyone who knew you. Tonight at St. A's we're having a party for you. No one is allowed to be sad … I'm wearing my red dress.

As she describes the memorial service, Adelaide's hands clutch at the material in the skirt of her dress. She seems unaware of what she is doing.

ADELAIDE   Tiny Shaw got a barbershop quartet together. They want to sing all your favourite songs. I told them they should sing "Pack Up Your Troubles" and "Katie" and "When You Wore a Tulip." Pause. I don't want them to sing the song about the sunrise. That's private.

Long pause then Adelaide sings:

Dear One, the world is waiting for the sunrise
Every rose is heavy with dew.

Stops singing and hums the last 3 lines. Addy's song is heard in the background during George's next speech.

Lights up on George.

GEORGE   I searched all night, you know. The wind blew out my lantern, but I kept going… Calling your name. Hoping… Hoping…

George reads the memorial card.

"Let thy faithful servant depart in peace." No peace for the ones you left behind, of course. This morning your mother kept apologizing to everyone for making them come out on such a stormy day. It'll be a while before that woman finds peace.

And Addy. She sent them a telegram. She wanted me to get … a blanket of wildflowers for your grave. "So people would remember how full of life…"

Pause.

Wildflowers in Saskatchewan in March! All the undertaker had were lilies. They looked like wax.

He sits down at the table.

Well, Addy doesn't have to know that.

He picks up a pen and begins to write:

The blanket of wildflowers you sent made a bright splash of colour in the snow... Roger's mother was touched that you remembered him. She says he was always such a reader that he didn't have many friends. She wanted you to have something to remember him by. I'm sending the cap he was wearing the last time you saw him...

ADELAIDE   We're all supposed to tell our favourite stories. I could tell about the day they brought you to St. A's. You were so alive ... and so angry. The air around you seemed charged — like the air before a thunderstorm. All the other volunteers were afraid to go near you. I was too. But that night when they turned out the lights, you asked me to stay. We sat in the dark for what seemed like an eternity. Finally you said, "I don't believe in anything any more." And I took your hand. You held on to mine so tight. Even when you fell asleep, I didn't want to let go. I'd never known anyone like you. There never was anyone like you.

You taught me so much, Roger — not just about soldiers and the war but also that there was a world outside of Toronto. Who could have known?

But my education still isn't complete. The last day at St. A's you promised you'd teach me how to say good-bye. I still have to learn how to do that.

Harmonica: "I'm Going to a Better Land"

END OF ACT I

ACT TWO

Scene 1

Lights up on Adelaide. She is wearing the red dress. In her hands is Roger's cap. It is apparent she has just received it.

ADELAIDE   "… his mother said he was always such a reader that he didn't have many friends."

She stops reading.

You had me, Roger. You had me.

She looks at the cap.

The day you left you looked so handsome in your uniform and this…

Adelaide reliving the scene the last day at St. A's

"A hat for the man who stands out in the crowd. One of a kind." Just like you. You had all the answers. Why weren't they enough? Why did you have to leave?

Lights up on George. He is coming in from chores.

GEORGE   Too soon for bed. If I go to sleep now, I wake up in the middle of the night. Nothing between a man and his thoughts at three a.m. Tiny Shaw always said the ache in the place where he lost his leg was the worst at three a.m.

– 37 –

During the following scenes, Roger is trying to break through to George and Adelaide, but for much of the Act it is as if he is separated from them by a glass wall.

GEORGE *(continuing)*   "Phantom pain" the doctor called it. The ache for what you have lost. They said it could last for years.

ROGER/OUT[3]   Years! I can't leave them like that. Aching for what they've lost — believing that what they lost had value. What did I ever give them but grief? Grief and ... words. So many words!

GEORGE   Talking to myself again. I've got to watch that. I've got to do something, or I'll go crazy. I should pack up Roger's books. Get them out of here. The Curries said, "Do what you like with them." Someone should get some use out of them.

He gets a box and starts putting books in it.

Considering what books did to Roger, maybe I should just burn them.

ROGER   Books didn't kill me, George.

GEORGE   I've never been much of a reader.

"Alfred Lord Tennyson." We did him at school.

He begins to read - again, mockingly and not very well.

> "Come, my friends,
> 'Tis not too late to seek a newer world.
> Push off, ..."

Blah! Blah! Blah!

> "... for my purpose holds
> To sail beyond the sunset, and the baths
> Of all the western stars, until I die."

ROGER *(to himself)*   I believed that once. When I was young, those words lifted me above the earth. I wanted to live forever.

GEORGE   Though much is taken, much abides; and though
We are not now that strength which in old days
Moved earth and heaven...,

---

3. In Act II, Roger is dead, but he participates in the action in two principal ways. First, as "ROGER/OUT" (i.e., Roger, out of the scene), he serves as an intimate choric figure, inaudible and invisible to Adelaide and George but important for the audience as he comments on action and also on his own posthumous spiritual journey. Secondly, Roger is embodied as Ben Cherendoff, Jack O'Neill, and as Adelaide's father. In each case, he is there to advance and encourage Adelaide and George on their journeys.

ROGER   "... that which we are, we are —
One equal temper of heroic hearts,
Made weak by time and fate, but strong in will
To strive, to seek, to find, and not to yield."[4]

Maybe it's not too late after all.

---

4. Alfred Lord Tennyson, *Ulysses*.

Scene 2

Adelaide still in her red dress, writing:

ADELAIDE   Roger took me into places I'd never been. Not real places. The only trip we ever took together was down to the corner to buy popcorn. But Roger made me see everything in a new way. Even my grandfather's house seemed different after I knew Roger.

I loved my grandfather's house on Yorkville Avenue. I loved the names of the big paintings that lined his halls: "Napoleon at Waterloo" and "The Charge of the Light Brigade" and "Nelson at Trafalgar" … . He loved everything about war. His library was full of books about military history, and he had whole battalions of tin soldiers. On rainy afternoons, Papa — that's what I called my grandfather — Papa and I used to kneel on the floor in front of the fireplace in his study and line the little soldiers up for battles. *She is silent, remembering.*

Papa taught me a poem. He told me the man in it was talking after a famous battle where many were killed, but the ones who were left were filled with pride. They lived heroically, he said, and that's what men must do.

> This story shall the good man teach his son
> And Crispin Crispian shall ne'er go by,
> From this day to the ending of the world,
> But we in it shall be remembered —
> We few, we happy few, we band of brothers.[5]

Pause

I never understood why only men could be heroes. I wanted to be one of the happy few. That's why I came here to St. A's. Then I met Roger.

When I met Roger at St. A's, he told me about our war, the Great War. It was not a story a good man would teach his sons and daughters. What Roger learned — what all of you

---

5. William Shakespeare, *King Henry V*, Act IV, Scene iii.

learned in the trenches of Belgium and France was the most terrible lesson a band of brothers has ever learned. You learned that war is trenches filled with stinking mud that sucks you in with every step so the rats gnaw your ankles and you can't escape the stench of chlorine gas and death.

Adelaide is losing control and Roger reaches out to her.

ROGER   Don't do this Addy.

ADELAIDE   He told me that books about military history belong on the garbage heap and that heroic paintings should be painted over by the men who've been to the front and know the truth. He told me that children must learn that in real wars, soldiers are made of flesh and blood, not tin, and that flesh can be torn and tortured, so that when men fall down they don't get up again. He taught me so much.

ROGER   Just the lessons of war Addy. There are other lessons…

Scene 3

Lights up on George reading Adelaide's letter.

GEORGE   I wish I'd been at your party, Addy... Come to think of it, I wish I was anywhere but here. Even after Mother and Dad died I loved this place. The horses, the cattle... the chickens...

He smiles remembering Roger

"Find my gas mask, McTaggart. Chickens beware..."

Now it's so dead here. The prospect of sitting in this room for the next 50 years...

Pause.   What was that line in Roger's book?

ROGER   Look it up, George. Remember the underlined parts are the significant ones. They're the lines I thought would be on the exam.

George gets the book and reads.

> "Come my friends, 'Tis not too late
> to seek a newer world."
> ... that which we are, we are —
> One equal temper of heroic hearts,
> Made weak by time and fate, but strong in will
> To strive, to seek, to find, and not to yield.

"Strive"? "Seek"? In Snipe Lake, Saskat-chewan?

Pause.

ROGER   But who says Snipe Lake is a life sentence?

GEORGE   We used to sing a song behind the lines, in the dugouts.

Roger plays: George sings

> We're here because we're here
> Because we're here, because we're here;
> We're here because we're here
> Because we're here, because we're here

ROGER   Enrico Caruso, it's good to hear you singing again.

George laughs   We're here because we're here... There should be more to life than that.

Picks up the book and continues reading.

Scene 4

Lights up on Adelaide writing.

ADELAIDE   George, I'm writing it all up. My memories of Roger. When the men talked about him the night of the party it was as if I had him back again. I'm going to take what I write to the newspaper and then everyone will know what a brave and fine man Roger Currie was.

ROGER/OUT You're making me sound like one of those apple-cheeked boys in *McTaggart's Book of Heroes*. The chaps at the front line had a verse:

> Though we observe the Higher Law
> And although we have our quarrel just,
> Were I permitted to withdraw
> You wouldn't see my arse for dust.

That was about it for my book.

ADELAIDE   I'll start with the story of how he saved Joe Messenger's life.

ROGER/OUT You'll have to re-write the ending. Make it a little more inspirational.

ADELAIDE   Maybe I should start earlier, with Roger growing up in Saskatoon.

ROGER/OUT Saskatoon, home of the heroes. Addy, don't do this. The world doesn't need another tin soldier.

He looks at her, wholly absorbed in her writing. Shouting —

Stop it, Addy! Don't waste your life.

She continues to write, oblivious. Finally, she picks up a newspaper, turns to the editorial page.

Adelaide reading The Toronto Examiner:

"And the truth shall make you free.[6]

Editor: Ben Cherendoff." Alright Mr. Cherendoff here I come.

---

6. John 8: 32.

ROGER/OUT Damn. For all the good I'm doing, I might as well be talking to the wall. Talk. That was always my specialty, wasn't it? Pause. In the army, they told us that if we couldn't achieve the target through direct assault, we should try subterfuge. Maybe it's time for action.

Roger picks up a cigar, sticks it in his mouth and exits.

Scene 5

Lights up. ROGER/OUT *as* BEN CHERENDOFF *is sitting behind the desk, chewing his cigar, reading Adelaide's article. Adelaide is standing in front of the desk, anxious.*

Adelaide clears her throat.

ROGER/OUT AS BEN *looks up at Adelaide*   You're still here.

ADELAIDE   I'm waiting to hear when you're going to publish my tribute to Roger Currie.

ROGER/OUT AS BEN   What'd you say your name was?

ADELAIDE   Adelaide, sir. Adelaide Farlinger.

ROGER/OUT AS BEN   Well, Adele, the short answer to your question is "Never." *The Examiner* is a newspaper. If you want to write pretty little memorials, learn to sew and make a sampler.

ADELAIDE   Thank you for your time. I'll take this across the street to *The Independent*.

ROGER/OUT AS BEN   Not so fast, Adele. Tell me, do you drink?

ADELAIDE   No.

ROGER AS BEN   How's your health?

ADELAIDE   I'm strong as an ox.

ROGER AS BEN   How're your legs?

ADELAIDE   I think my ankles are a bit thick, but apart from that…

ROGER AS BEN   Adele, do I look like a lecher to you?

ADELAIDE   No, sir.

ROGER AS BEN   Now think about this for a minute, Adele. Is there any reason other than hanky-panky that an editor might ask a person he's thinking of hiring how her legs are?

ADELAIDE   Thinking of hiring, sir?

ROGER AS BEN   Thinking of hiring, Adele. Now, I get a turn again. Why do you think I asked about your legs?

ADELAIDE   To see if I have stamina, sir?

Mike Stack as Roger/Ben, Burgandy Code as Adelaide Farlinger

ROGER AS BEN   Right. Good. Adele, you can pick up your ten-cent cigar on your way out of the office. Now, you may have noticed that we're not *The New York Times*. Joseph Pulitzer would not be happy to hear it, but at this newspaper, legs are more important than brains. I haven't got the savoir faire or the bucks to pay debutantes to write little columns while they're waiting for their dance cards to fill up. Adele, you work for me, you work. Eight a.m. to six p.m., and nights if one of the guys is sick or drunk and that's every night. I'm going to take a chance on you. Your subject matter wasn't quite what we're after, but you've got a nice way with words and we could use some young blood around here. You start tomorrow.

ADELAIDE   I haven't said I wanted the job, sir.

ROGER AS BEN   Take it, Adele. Don't miss the chance.

ROGER/OUT *(turns to us)*   *Carpe diem.* Seize the day. That's what my Latin teacher, Miss Violet, tried to teach me. Why did it take me so long to learn?

Scene 6

Lights up on Adelaide writing.

ADELAIDE   Mr. Cherendoff seems so sure I'll take the job, George. But I'm not. Roger was the clever one. He was the one who'd read all the books and knew all the answers.

Lights up on George.

GEORGE   He didn't have all the answers, Addy.

ADELAIDE   It should have been Roger's job. He would have been brilliant. He could have put everything people our age feel into words, so that everyone would understand.

GEORGE   You can do that, Addy. You may not have read all the books, but you have a heroic heart.

ADELAIDE   I'm no hero, George.

GEORGE   You're still here.

Long pause. Lights down on Adelaide.

And so am I. How am I going to find answers, living with ghosts and listening to the parlour clock?

That poem about Ulysses was like a bucket of cold water in my face. Sliv Mitchell would be glad to rent this place again. He had her running smooth as a top when I was overseas.

He stands.   It's decided. I'm leaving.

ROGER   Would a veteran of the Blind and Halt Platoon be welcome on the journey?

GEORGE   "Come my friends, 'tis not too late to seek a newer world
... my purpose holds
To sail beyond the sunset, and the baths
Of all the western stars."

ROGER   "To seek... to find..."

GEORGE   I've always wanted to visit Winnipeg!

Roger picks up his harmonica and begins to play "How're ya gonna keep 'em down on the farm, after they've seen Paree?"

Scene 7

Lights up on Adelaide at a typewriter. There is a litter of paper around her. She obviously is having a hard time writing her article.

ADELAIDE *(reads what she has just written)*   Last night at the Grand Opera House, The Canadian musical group the Dumbells said thanks to a special group of men. The song and joke troop declared tickets to their performance were free to returned soldiers, and the theatre was packed. Many of the men had last seen the Dumbells during the heat of battle. Now these returned soldiers are back in Toronto, getting on with their lives, looking forward to the future they fought for. No one wanted the evening to end. The soldiers stayed outside the Grand Theatre until two in the morning, talking and remembering. Grateful to be home safe.

'Home safe.' *She crumples up the page.*

Lies.

I can't do this.

BEN   Can't do what?

ADELAIDE   I can't write fairy tales.

Ben reads what she has written.

ROGER AS BEN   Soldiers. Home. Happy times ahead. Our readers'll eat it up, Adele. Besides, I thought from that piece you wrote about your friend Roger Currie, you were partial to romantic images.

ADELAIDE   What I wrote about Roger that first day was true. He was…

Roger as Ben holds a hand up to stem the flow.

ADELAIDE   Roger was brave and brilliant. That was the truth. But this isn't. Or at least it's only partly true.

ROGER AS BEN/ROGER AS ROGER   What is the truth?

ADELAIDE   The Dumbells were wonderful. All the jokes and the old songs. And the audience did have a wonderful time.

That part's true. But those men didn't stay out on the street until two in the morning because they couldn't bear to have the evening end. A lot of them stayed because they didn't have a place to go.

Mr. Cherendoff, do you know that a bathroom flat costs as much as an 8 or 9 room house did before the war. And even if those men are lucky enough to find a flat, most of them can't pay for it, because they don't have jobs.

The men out in front of that theatre were angry, Mr. Cherendoff. They feel as if they've been betrayed. I don't understand what's happening.

ROGER AS BEN   You know Adele, politics as usual.

ADELAIDE   But isn't politics about the Grits wanting reciprocity and the Tories saying we're selling Canada to the United States? This is about men who want jobs and homes and families. All through the war, our government kept saying how proud we were of our men. If we were so proud of them, then, why are we turning our backs on them now?

ROGER AS BEN   Sometimes, it's hard to face the fact that we've failed people. Keep asking questions, Addy. I never asked enough questions. Maybe I was afraid of what I'd hear.

Scene 8

Lights up on George writing.

GEORGE   I've done it. Look at that postmark, Addy. Winnipeg, Manitoba! I rented the farm, caught the train, and here I am.

"Come my friends, 'tis not too late to seek a newer world." That's what I did, and what a world I've found. Addy, I wish you were here. That typewriter of yours would be clacking away night and day: new places, new people, new experiences. The first night I was here I went down to Market Square behind the City Hall. Now there's a place that gets your brain cells moving: Weight lifters, evangelists, suffragettes, Royalists, Anti-Royalists, supporters of the single tax system, opponents of the single tax system, salvationists, anarchists — and a Professor of Phrenological and Mental Sciences who, for only the quarter part of a dollar, offered to feel the bumps on my head and predict my future.

Addy, I was so overwhelmed, I thought I really must need my head read for leaving the farm.

Then I met Jack O'Neill.

George and Roger as Jack are in scene.

ROGER AS JACK   REFORMERS, REVIVERS, REDEEMERS, and RENOUNCERS!

GEORGE   How can all of these people seem so certain that the answers they've come up with are the right ones?

ROGER AS JACK   Now that's something to look out for. Beware of the man-or the woman- who has a plan that can solve every problem and wipe every tear.

GEORGE   I've always thought any man worth his salt has to come up with his own answers.

ROGER AS JACK   And you were right.

* * *

Left to right: Mike Stack as Roger/Jack, Tom Roonie as George

GEORGE *(writing to Addy)*   I've seen things I thought I'd never see in Canada: families living in shacks, kids who are sick and dirty; people starving… starving in the world's bread basket.

ROGER AS JACK *(in mid-sentence)*   It's got to stop! There are but two classes in Canada: the Idle and the Industrious. Now ask yourself, who enjoys the fruits of our labour, but denies us a decent place to live.

If someone doesn't turn it around soon, there could be bloodshed.

GEORGE *(looking hard at him)*   There has to be another way.

ROGER AS JACK   Then don't just sit on the sidelines twiddling your thumbs. Look for that other way before it's too late.

Lights down on Roger.

GEORGE *(writing to Addy)* More and more I hear talk of a strike, Addy.

The men I've been talking to say it's time everyone walked out. They think things are so bad now they can only win if God Himself joins their side. They play a kind of hymn at their meetings. I forget all the words but part of it goes:

Sings, with Roger [to the tune of "My Old Kentucky Home"]:

> Then we'll sing one song of the One Big Union Grand
> The hope of the toiler and slave,
> It's coming fast; it is sweeping sea and land,
> To the terror of the grafter and the knave

ROGER/OUT   Well done, Enrico Caruso.

Scene 9

Lights up on Adelaide confronting Roger as Ben.

ADELAIDE   Ben, how can I write a story about a hen who lays double-yolked eggs?

ROGER AS BEN   Come on, Adele. It's a nice seasonal article. No use making people uncomfortable by asking questions nobody has answers for.

ADELAIDE   Then where will the answers come from?

ROGER AS BEN   Better to ruffle feathers than to immortalize double-yokers?

ADELAIDE   Yes, I think it's our job to ruffle feathers. I keep seeing faces, Ben. The men I talked to outside the Grand Opera house the night the Dumbells were here. The families my friend, George, told me about: mothers with dead eyes, sick, hungry children, desperate fathers. So many people in pain, Ben. Do you think they're interested in reading about a chicken who lays double-yolked eggs?

ROGER AS BEN   They're not the ones who buy the papers Adele.

ADELAIDE   That doesn't mean they don't count.

She moves towards the window.

Come here, Ben, just for a minute. Look out there. What do you see?

ROGER AS BEN   I see the offices of Soldiers' Civil Re-establishment.

ADELAIDE   What else?

ROGER AS BEN   I see the coat of arms of the Dominion of Canada over the door, and I see the Union Jack snapping in the breeze.

ADELAIDE   And...?

ROGER AS BEN   I see men waiting.

The politicians would say times are tough everywhere.

ADELAIDE   Then damn the politicians! What's happening to this country? Tomorrow is April 9th — two years ago the Canadian volunteers captured Vimy Ridge. Remember how proud we all were? We had a special chapel at my school, and we cheered till our throats ached. Miss NacNaughton, our principal, said that Canada had done what no other nation could — turned the tide of the war. She said that we must always remember that Easter Monday 1917 was the day Canada came of age as a nation.

Pause.   I'm not going to write about that chicken, Ben.

ROGER AS BEN   What do you propose to write about, Adele?

ADELAIDE   I don't know, Ben. I might write about those men out there. I might write about the politicians who are betraying them. Who knows - I might even write about Vimy.

ROGER/OUT   That typewriter of yours will change more lives that I ever did.

Roger steps out of scene and turns to the audience.

ROGER AS BEN   She's a firebrand. Listen carefully, and you'll hear the fountain pens of the Righteous being uncapped all over Toronto.

Scene 10

Lights up on George reading Addy's Vimy column.

GEORGE   Remembering Vimy

"April 9th, 1919: Two years ago today, Easter Monday, 1917, 80,000 Canadians marched on Vimy Ridge. The Canadians suffered 10,602 casualties in the battle, including 3,598 dead, but the Ridge was taken by noon. Some say the capture of Vimy Ridge turned the tide of the war. Some say April 9th, 1917, was the day that Canada came of age, that on that day, we, as a nation, took the first step towards that 'better land' that our soldiers sang about and dreamed of and risked their youth and their lives for."

ADELAIDE   "Yesterday, I went to the office of the Soldiers' Civil Reestablishment on Church Street. I wanted to talk with some men who'd been at Vimy Ridge. I wanted to hear what they thought about the country they've come home to.

The office is a busy place. Returned men spill out into the hallway from a reception area that seems to have forgotten its purpose. The young men are everywhere. They sit and smoke. And they wait: for news of a job; for word of a decent place to live that doesn't cost the moon; for some sign, however small, that our government at least knows they exist."

GEORGE   "'Tired of waiting' — that's the phrase you hear again and again. When the Great War came, these men put aside their jobs, their sweethearts, and their plans. They did it proudly and without question. These men are heroes, but they are not asking for a hero's medal. Most of them have medals enough. What they want are jobs. They are tired of waiting. Beneath the banter there is an undercurrent of anger."

ADELAIDE   "And I am telling you, the readers of *The Examiner*, that anger is growing.

I am not a politician, but I believe that if we allow the anger of our returned men to grow unchecked, our young nation will have a battle on her hands that will make Vimy Ridge look like child's play. This time, all Canadians will be numbered among the wounded."

GEORGE   Oh, Addy, this column is going to explode like a bombshell.

George picks up a pen and begins to write.

But you wrote all the right things, and it's about time people heard the truth. Remember Roger talking about that Greek chap, Dioga-something, who walked all over the world with his lamp, looking for an honest person. Well, Dioga-whatever could have stopped when he found you. Oh Addy I am so proud of you. That's a stupid thing to say to a grown woman, but it's the truth. I am proud of you. I'm writing too. I'm keeping a journal. Don't laugh. I know it's more the kind of thing Roger would do than what you would expect from me, but I'm finding that if I work at it, I can get straight how I feel about things. So much is happening in Winnipeg that I need the chance to get my thinking organized. No easy feat!

I don't know what I'd do without Jack. We're not at all alike, and sometimes he frightens me, the way Roger could when he got into one of his moods.

ROGER AS JACK   Are you still stuck into that journal, McTaggart? What are you writing about today?

GEORGE   Questions — questions without answers. One minute, I think being in Winnipeg is improving my eyesight. The next, I'm seeing so many things that it's all a blur…

ROGER AS JACK   Must be the famous Manitoba sunshine!

GEORGE   Maybe. Maybe I'm just finally doing what my friend Roger urged me to do.

ROGER   Take the blinkers off.

GEORGE *(startled)*   How did you… ?

ROGER AS JACK *(quickly)*   And this Roger chap? Where is he now?

GEORGE   He's dead.

ROGER AS JACK   Ah, a casualty of the war, was he?

GEORGE   Yes, I guess you could say that.

Pause   He took his own life.

ROGER AS JACK   And are you looking for something inspirational in that decision?

GEORGE   Roger was my closest friend! We went through hell together and survived!

ROGER AS JACK   Only one of you survived, George.

Jack reaches into his pocket and pulls out a much unfolded and refolded sheet of paper. He unfolds the paper and hands it to George.

GEORGE   What's this?

ROGER AS JACK   A poem. I'd be grateful if you read it. Hear the words, George.

George reacts for a moment to this echo of Roger, and then reads:

       "'Tis not too late to seek a newer world..."

I'm just one man. What can I do?

ROGER AS JACK   One man alone? Not much. He's just a target. But two men marching down the middle of the street at midnight singing — that's a parade.

GEORGE *(reacts to the resonance)*   Do you believe in ghosts, Jack?

ROGER AS JACK   Of course I do. I'm an Irishman!

GEORGE   But what do you believe? What are they?

ROGER AS JACK   What's troublin' you, lad?

GEORGE   I have a ghost, Jack.

ROGER AS JACK   Ah yes, that's entirely possible, it is! And do you recognize your ghost? Could it be your dead friend?

GEORGE   Yes. It's Roger. He hasn't really died. I can still feel him close to me. Does that make sense?

ROGER AS JACK   It does. Why do you suppose your friend's spirit is so restless?

GEORGE   I don't know. Maybe there was more he wanted to say.

ROGER AS JACK   Or something more you should be doing.

Scene 11

Lights up on Adelaide. She is writing a letter to George and she is very upset.

ADELAIDE   George, for the first time in my life I'm absolutely alone. It's the Vimy article, of course. I knew it would cause an uproar, but I didn't have any choice.

Everybody but Ben is angry with me. The mailroom at the paper is filled with letters calling me a "Bolshy" and threatening to cancel their subscriptions. My father came down to *The Examiner* this morning and told Ben that if I wasn't forced to write a retraction, he and his friends would cancel their advertising.

ROGER/OUT *to audience*   A battalion of Uncle Williams against one nineteen-year-old woman.

ADELAIDE   Ben just laughed at him, but I was furious. When I found out, I went straight to my father's office.

ROGER   Fight the good fight, Addy. Snatch victory from the jaws of the old men.

Roger/Out picks up a vest and moves into the scene as Mr. Farlinger.

ADELAIDE   How dare you come down to the paper. How dare you interfere. I love you Father, I respect you, but this is not the Dark Ages. This is 1919, and I have the right to live my own life.

ROGER AS MR. FARLINGER   Not when you expose your family to shame by writing treasonous lies. Lies fed you by those malcontents you consort with at the Hospital.

ADELAIDE   Father, what I wrote is not a lie. It is the truth, and no one fed it to me. I discovered it for myself. She picks up a newspaper. In today's paper, Ben printed some pictures of people I found on the streets of Toronto. Look. Returned soldiers begging for handouts. Families living in shacks.

She holds the newspaper out to him. He snatches it out of her hand.

ROGER AS MR. FARLINGER   I don't read filth, Adelaide. And I'll not have you walking the streets of Toronto like a harlot. Do you hear me? I'll not have it. And, Adelaide, I won't have you working for a Jew. You're a Farlinger, and it's time you remembered that. Choose, Adelaide. Live in my house as my daughter, or forever cast your lot with that rag tag bunch of lowlifes you seem to have grown so fond of.

ADELAIDE   I have no choice, father. I'll be out of your house by six o'clock tonight.

ROGER AS MR. FARLINGER   Then I no longer have a daughter.

ADELAIDE   And I no longer have a father.

Roger moves out of the scene.

ROGER/OUT *(to Adelaide)*   More loss. How many hearts are broken by closed minds? How many hearts did I break because I was too busy sniping to listen?

Scene 12

GEORGE There's a thunderstorm coming. You can almost feel the electricity in the air.

Jack, I was just down on Portage and Main with some chaps who'd been over in Belgium. Maybe half of a dozen of us — not many. Two of Thompson's "Specials" were on duty.

ROGER AS JACK Vicious bastards they are too.

GEORGE A couple of our fellows started to taunt them — just jeers, nothing more than you could hear at any softball tournament. But the Specials turned on us. They chased us. They smashed one of our men on the head with a club. Did you hear what I just said? "One of our men." But the Specials are our men too. We're not even in a war.

Why does there have to be bloodshed?

Jack, I'm twenty-three. I spent sixteen months in the middle of a nightmare dreamed up by people who believed somebody else's bloodshed was the answer. I believe in the cause of the workers. I really do. But I can't believe in the violence anymore. There has to be another way.

ROGER AS JACK Maybe you should run for Parliament, McTaggart.

GEORGE You know, Jack, maybe I should.

ROGER AS JACK *laughs* Well, you've got my vote. Oh here's another vote you've got. Some reporter from Toronto brought it by the Y.

He sniffs the letter.

It smelled better than this when it got delivered.

Roger waves the letter high in the air. The two men grapple good naturedly for the letter. Finally Roger/Jack hands it over. George tears the letter out of its envelope.

ROGER AS JACK Easy, boyo, I have a feeling that's a letter you should pay attention to.

GEORGE *reads*: "… For the first time in my life, I'm absolutely alone." You're not alone, Addy. You have me. Whenever you want.

And I think it's time I told you so.

He takes a stub of pencil from his pocket and begins writing on a page from his notebook:

I guess if you were brave enough to take on all of Toronto with your Vimy column, I should be brave enough to tell you how I feel about you. So here it is in plain English:

Addy, I care about you very much. When I look back, I think I've always felt this way about you. I never said anything because of Roger. But Roger's gone now, and I wonder if it's possible that I have a chance. Whatever you decide, please know this. As long as I am alive, you will never be alone.

Scene 13

Lights up on Adelaide with the letter in her hand.

This is the low point for Adelaide. She picks up a pen and begins to write.

ADELAIDE   I don't think love is possible for me anymore. I've started having the most terrible dream. I'm on the bank of a river. It's big and powerful. I have a child with me — a little girl. I know I'm supposed to care for her, but I hear Roger calling me. He's in such agony, and I run to help him. I search and search, but I can't find him. And then I'm back on the riverbank, but the little girl is gone. When I look down into the water, I can see her — the current is carrying her away. I dive into the water and bring her out. Very gently, I lay her down on the riverbank. That's when I see that the child's face is my face.

George, I always wake up before I know whether the little girl is still alive. What if she isn't? What if the part of me you remember and care for is dead?

Dearest friend, you deserve the best girl in the world. With all my heart I hope you find her.

Lights up on George.

GEORGE   I have found her, Addy. And I'm not going to walk away. We've already had one desertion...

ROGER/OUT *struck by the insight*   It was desertion, wasn't it?

GEORGE   This platoon can't take another loss... It's time we closed the ranks. I'm coming to Toronto.

ROGER/OUT   March forth. There's no deserting this time.

Scene 14

George is standing outside Adelaide's door. He's holding a package wrapped in newspapers: fish and chips. Roger is again on the periphery, listening, reacting. Addy enters. At first she doesn't see George, but he sees her and he's shocked by the change in her. When, finally, she does notice him, she's so tense she jumps back from him.

GEORGE   Addy, it's alright. It's me, George.

ADELAIDE   George, what are you doing in Toronto? You did get my letter, didn't you? The one where I told you that…

GEORGE   I'm not here as a suitor, Addy. Just as a friend. I thought it was time for a reunion of the Blind and Halt Platoon… Look, I even brought dinner: fish and chips.

ADELAIDE   How did you know I'd be home?

GEORGE   I didn't, but Addy, I'd rather eat cold fish and chips with you than pheasant under glass at the Royal York with any other girl in Toronto.

They enter Addy's room.

Adelaide looks about as if she's seeing the room for the first time.

ADELAIDE   It's a mess, isn't it? I work all day and usually I have dinner at St. A's.

Tiny Shaw's convinced I'll die if I eat my own cooking. He's probably right. Anyway, I guess I haven't made this place very welcoming.

GEORGE   It looks fine to me. You look fine to me. Your hair's different.

ADELAIDE   I decided to cut it all off.

GEORGE   A kid at Snipe Lake School had hair like that.

Pause.   He was the best shortstop I ever saw… come on, we'd better eat our dinner before it gets cold.

He clears off the table, looking at Roger's cap for a beat before he moves it. They eat. Adelaide hungrily, George hardly at all. He can't take his eyes off her.

ADELAIDE   I'd forgotten how good food can be.

GEORGE   I'll bring you fish and chips every night.

ADELAIDE   If I ate like this every night, I'd start to look like matron.

Adelaide picks up Roger's cap. She doesn't appear to notice what she's done. Throughout the scene, she holds the cap. At first she holds the cap tenderly. As she becomes angry at George, she twists it in agitation. Finally when she says "damn you" to Roger, she throws the cap across the room.

ADELAIDE   Remember what Tiny Shaw used to call her bosom?

GEORGE   "No Man's Land." And Roger said, "Even Lord Kitchener wouldn't dare send a soldier in to claim it!"

They both laugh.

ADELAIDE   That's the first time that's happened.

GEORGE   What?

ADELAIDE   That I've remembered Roger and been able to smile.

GEORGE   It hasn't been easy for you, has it?

ADELAIDE   I didn't know anything could hurt this much.

Pause.

GEORGE   Addy, were you ever mad at Roger for what he did?

ADELAIDE   Of course, not. How could I be angry?

GEORGE   I was mad. If you want the truth, I was furious. I thought he was a coward to leave.

ADELAIDE   No. He was the bravest man I know. When I listened to him talk about how we have to change the world, I was brave too…

GEORGE   My mother used to say…

ADELAIDE   I don't want to hear what your mother said.

GEORGE   She used to say, "A man of words and not of deeds is like a garden full of weeds." Roger didn't change the world, Addy. He just left it.

ADELAIDE   Stop it, George. I'm not going to listen to this. He had to leave. He had no choice.

GEORGE   He had a choice Addy. A lot of men didn't, but Roger did, and he chose to die. It was hard for me to forgive him for that.

ADELAIDE   Don't you dare talk of forgiveness.

You're the one who needs forgiveness for saying these things. He had a brilliant mind, George. He was heroic. He went into the darkness alone.

GEORGE   I'd swallow a lot to keep you from being mad at me, but I can't swallow this. Roger was no hero. He was just a man who decided he didn't want to live anymore.

ADELAIDE   You have no right to judge him.

GEORGE   I'm not judging him, Addy. I'm just saying we shouldn't make him out to be something he wasn't.

ADELAIDE   No!

GEORGE *(very quietly)*   Did he say goodbye to you, Addy?

Silence.

Did he? Did he have the simple decency to tell you he was leaving?

ADELAIDE *(breaking)*   No, he never told me. Long silence. He never thought about me at all.

All he thought about was himself. His pain. His darkness. I didn't matter.

He didn't even care enough to say goodbye. She throws the cap across the stage. Damn you, Roger. Damn you to hell. You never even said goodbye...

As Adelaide sobs, Roger reaches out to comfort her, but she turns away from him. It is George who puts his arms around her and draws her to him. After a long while, George speaks.

GEORGE   The last time I held you like this was at St. A's.

ADELAIDE   Sod Buster's Ballroom. All those afternoons I made you dance... You hated waltzing so much.

GEORGE   My leg's a lot stronger because of that waltzing. Pause. Addy, maybe some night I could return the favour and take you dancing.

Adelaide is silent.

GEORGE   I guess that wasn't such a good idea.

If you're alright now, I'd better get my things over to the Y.

ADELAIDE   Stay here, George, please ... I don't want to be alone tonight.

GEORGE   Addy, I'll stay with you for as long as you want.

ROGER/OUT   That night, George sat with Addy and held her hand until she fell asleep, just as she had held my hand during those endless nights when I first came to St. A's. I should have been the one to return the favour… But George had earned the right to be there:

Remember what he said *(mockingly)*: "Even when the burden gets heavy, a Canadian boy doesn't walk away." Words to live by … Maybe they really were.

Scene 15

Lights up on George.

GEORGE   I thought this morning I'd go across to the university again.

ADELAIDE *(laughing)*   You're been there every day for two weeks. Soon, they'll have to give you a degree.

GEORGE   I don't think it works that way. But I don't care. I'm happy just being there. When I was a kid I used to like to sit in our hayloft. It was so peaceful just watching the light come through the cracks between the boards, thinking, dreaming.

After Roger died, I was sure I'd never want to be alone with my thoughts again. But there's something about the way the light pours in through the windows at Victoria College... And the library. There must be a hundred thousand books there. Addy, in those stacks there are answers to questions I haven't even thought of yet. If I'm going to make any changes, I'll have to do a lot of reading and a lot of learning.

Adelaide smiles.

You're laughing at me.

ADELAIDE   I'm just thinking how amazed Roger would be to hear all this.

GEORGE   He could never understand why I didn't love books the way he did. The hours I spent reading to him and the hours he spent yelling at me about how badly I read.

ADELAIDE *(doing a pretty fair Roger imitation)* "McTaggart,   you have the emotional range of a seventh grade student reading from the B.N.A. Act. Get some feeling into it man. These writers are speaking to you from beyond the grave."

GEORGE *(laughing)*   He's never far from us, is he? I wish he'd had his chance Addy. I wish he was starting University with me in September. I used to think he knew so much about life. But I'm beginning to see he only knew about one part of life, and it wasn't the best part.

Adelaide moves toward George. She is genuinely struck by his insight. There's a moment when they almost connect, but she's not ready.

There's a University of Saskatchewan calendar on the table in front of them, and Adelaide picks it up. It is clear she has been knocked off base by this truth about Roger.

ADELAIDE   Your calendar from the University came. Look at all these courses. Have you decided what you're going to take?

GEORGE   I thought I'd begin with Chemistry, English Literature, European History, Philosophy, and Greek.

ADELAIDE   What would you ever do with Greek?

GEORGE *(happily)*   I don't know.

ADELAIDE   I have some news too. Ben asked me to go on the Prince of Wales Tour. The reporter who was supposed to go came down with influenza. Ben wanted me to replace him.

GEORGE   Addy, that's the chance of a lifetime. The Prince of Wales will be the next king of England. You'll be hobnobbing with royalty. Of course, he's the lucky one. He'll be hobnobbing with you.

ADELAIDE   I'm afraid there's not going to be any hobnobbing, George. I told Ben "No."

Adelaide moves into the scene with Roger as Ben.

ROGER AS BEN   What d'you mean 'No,' Adele. This isn't an excursion to Newtonville to interview a guy who's grown a potato that looks like the Prime Minister. This is the Prince of Wales Tour — Halifax to Vancouver — coast to coast, east to west, sea to shining sea.

ADELAIDE   No, Ben, I'm not ready. I don't know enough.

ROGER AS BEN   Spell *crepe de chine*, Adele.

ADELAIDE   *c-r-e-p-e d-e c-h-i-n-e*

ROGER AS BEN   Now spell *peau-de-soie*.

ADELAIDE   *p-e-a-u d-e s-o-i-e*.

ROGER AS BEN   You know enough. The wives of half the mayors will be wearing *crepe de chine* and the other half will be wearing *peau de soie*. Be at Union Station 7:30 Wednesday morning.

ADELAIDE   No, I don't belong there, Ben.

ROGER AS BEN   It's exactly where you belong, Addy. Travelling with a Prince, while all of Canada spreads out before you, like a magnificent Persian carpet that will carry you on adventures you can't even dream of now.

Adelaide should react to the "Addy" and to this allusion to what she told Roger back at St. A's. Then she should turn back to George.

ADELAIDE   It would be a wonderful chance George. I know that. But I'm afraid.

GEORGE   Of what?

ADELAIDE   I'm afraid to leave. As long as I can go to St. A's for dinner and talk to Tiny or just stand by the window in the sunroom and look down at the street and see what "all the common folk are doing," Roger is still alive in me. I haven't closed the door.

GEORGE   It's time, Addy. Time to close the door.

ADELAIDE   "Time Gentlemen." I remember Roger saying that his last day at St. A's. "Time to leave the warmth and go out into the cold cruel world."

GEORGE   It doesn't have to be cruel Addy. Now come on, we'll spend today doing all the things we like best, starting with breakfast at Childs': let's order the most expensive breakfast on the menu, the one that has the muskmelon cut into those little boat things. He takes her hand. We'd better get started. Remember, we have to have you at Union Station by seven sharp, tomorrow morning. It wouldn't be right to keep the Prince waiting.

Adelaide touches his cheek and says very quietly.

No, a Prince shouldn't have to wait.

ROGER/OUT *to us*   Oh Addy, you are worth waiting for.

Scene 16

The Tour:

George sitting at a table stacked with notebooks, a jam-jar of pencils, the kinds of forms a university student must wrestle with at the beginning of term. At the moment, none of this seems to hold much interest for him. His attention is wholly on the picture in his hand and in the letter which accompanied it.

Lights up on Adelaide. We see the real thing.

ADELAIDE   I'm in Halifax. I talked the photographer from the Star into taking this picture. Since you're responsible for my being here, I don't want you to miss a minute of the adventure, even if you are burning the midnight oil out there in Saskatoon. I borrowed the trousers I'm wearing from an American reporter. According to her, they're all the rage in New York City. She says when I wear them, I look as if I just stepped off a magazine cover. I think I probably look more like that shortstop you knew in Snipe Lake.

This morning we climbed over the shoulder of the peninsula to see where the explosion of 1917 had taken place. It is a terrible sight — burned out houses and ragged grass on hillsides so deeply scarred you think they'll never heal.

Roger told me once he thought the Halifax explosion was ... a perfect metaphor for the war. It started by accident, but the force of the explosion levelled everything in its wake.

I used that idea as the lead in my story. I'm proud of that article, George. I think Roger would be proud of it too.

GEORGE *reads the Itinerary*:

TUES. August 19 — Arrive Charlottetown, P.E.I.

THURS. August 21 — Arrive Quebec City.

SUN. August 24 — Depart Quebec City: The Royal Train

MON. August 25 - Arrive Toronto, Ontario.

Lights up Adelaide.

ADELAIDE   Toronto. The Prince came to St. A's today. It seemed so strange to walk up our old path and see the future King of England a few steps ahead of me.

There was such a crush in the sunroom that I had to stay outside in the hall. I was standing by the door, listening to the Prince make his speech, when I heard him say:

"And who is Adelaide?"

My knees began to shake.

Then Tiny Shaw said, "She's a young woman who served King and Country with great distinction, Your Highness and she's a member of the press corps covering your visit to Canada." I squeezed past the others and Tiny presented me.

Adelaide is in the scene.

ADELAIDE *curtsies*   Your Royal Highness.

Pause.   The Prince reached out to shake my hand. His eyes were as blue as forget-me-nots. The flashbulbs were popping all around me. Everyone wanted to get a picture of the sign the men of Ward 8 had made:

WELCOME
to
TWO OF THE BEST:
ADELAIDE
AND
THE PRINCE

I looked around the room and the men were beaming. They were so proud of themselves, but not as proud as I was. Then everyone went to the parlour for tea, and I was alone … alone in our old den of iniquity.

ADELAIDE   Time to say goodbye.

Adelaide walks to the window and looks out.

Do you want to hear what the common folk are doing today, Roger? George is off in Saskatoon. He's going to start university next week. And tomorrow morning I'm getting on a train that will take me clear across Canada. I'm going to the Rockies, my love. I'm going to see your mountains. The surviving members of the Platoon are going on.

ROGER   Godspeed.

ADELAIDE   Oh Roger, I can't.

ROGER   Please Addy, you don't need me anymore.

ADELAIDE   I can't leave you behind.

He holds his hand out to her, but she doesn't see it. She turns from him and walks away.

ROGER   Then I'll have to go with you. He follows.

Scene 17

George sitting at his desk. His textbooks now have covers, obviously handmade from newspapers. Roger is in this scene. By the end of George's speech we know Roger is beginning to find a measure of peace.

GEORGE   I couldn't believe my eyes when I opened the Saskatoon *Phoenix* last week and saw you and the Prince grinning out at me. What do you think Roger would have made of the moment? I think he — would have been torn — on the one hand, furious that the King's son "was riding around in luxury while Canadian boys couldn't find jobs"; on the other, very proud of you for giving the men at St. A's such a moment.

I'm not torn at all. I'm just proud of you. As soon as I saw the photo I went up and down 9th Street and begged my neighbours to save their newspapers. I've covered all my texts in the section with your photo — Your beauty encloses *Classical Literature*, *Bates Chemistry*, *Paradise Lost*, Thomas MacCauley's *History of England*, two terrifying looking Mathematics texts and my prize possesion, Roger's copy of *Thucydides*.

I can't get enough of this book. I don't know a word of Greek, but when I look at these mysterious marks on the pages I feel like the old Greeks are sending me messages. I can't wait to decode them.

George reads the name on the first page of the book.

"Roger Allan Currie." You're still pushing me, Roger. Still urging me to try new things. When we were overseas it was the blood pudding at the World's End. I'd never seen such a thing, but it was pretty good.

ROGER   And *As You Like It*. After all your grousing, you admitted you even liked Shakespeare a bit too.

GEORGE   Even now you're pushing me into new worlds. I'm a farm boy, you know. My Mum and Dad were the finest people on earth, but the idea that their son would attend university would have been as strange to them as the thought that I would fly to the moon.

Yet next week I begin classes. It never would have happened without you, Roger. I'll be grateful to you for that and more, till the day I die.

ROGER   No, George, in the end, you'll be the one who will make things right.

GEORGE *picks up Addy's itinerary and reads*:   Now   let's   see... how long I have to wait.

MONDAY, September 8 — Arrive Port Arthur and Fort William, Ontario

TUESDAY, September 9 — Arrive Winnipeg, Manitoba

500 miles. Five hundred miles!

ROGER   Finally, Saskatoon.

Scene 18

Lights up on Adelaide and George rushing toward one another. They embrace, break apart and stand looking at one another. Roger is, as usual, outside the circle.

GEORGE AND ADELAIDE *together*   You look wonderful.
It's so good to see you.

ADELAIDE   It really is good to see you George. It's like coming home.

GEORGE   I'm always here.

ADELAIDE   I know. *Pause.* Now, tell me all about university and where you're living and the people you've met. Have you made any new friends?

GEORGE   A few… Addy, there's news of our old friends.

ADELAIDE   Nothing's happened to…

GEORGE   Everyone's fine. It's just they're tearing down St. A's. I had a letter from Tiny Shaw this morning.

ADELAIDE   Tiny never said anything about it to me.

GEORGE   He didn't want to spoil your homecoming.

ADELAIDE   I can't imagine a world without St. A's. *Pause.* Did I ever tell you about my first day there? It was a disaster. I spilled a bedpan, tipped a patient out of his wheelchair and dropped a whole tray of thermometers. There was glass and mercury all over the floor. Then to top it all off, I scalded poor Tiny when I gave him a sponge bath.

GEORGE   I'll bet you heard some choice language then.

ADELAIDE   No, he was very nice. He held out the corner of his sheet and said "Here, blow your nose and give us a smile. You don't have to be perfect for us. All we care about is that you're here…"

GEORGE   I still feel that way about you, Addy.

George and Adelaide come together. They embrace. Roger moves between them separating them.

ADELAIDE   I guess if we're going to visit Roger's grave, we'd better go. The Prince's tour leaves in two hours.

George and Adelaide leave together, with Roger following.

Tom Roonie as George McTaggart, Burgandy Code as Adelaide Farlinger

* * *

In the darkness

ROGER *reads*   September 12, Edmonton
  September 14, Calgary
  September 16, High River, Alberta.

Scene 19

Lights up on Adelaide.

ADELAIDE   I've had the strangest experience. It's about Roger. When we stood by Roger's grave on the river bank I felt such pain. As we moved west through Alberta, I carried that pain with me. It was as if a vise were squeezing my heart.

Monday morning we drove out to a cattle ranch at a place called High River. It was there that I got my first view of the Rockies, "Roger's mountains." We had lunch and then everyone was searching out boots and hats and cameras so we could photograph the Prince branding cattle. I was just heading out the door —

ROGER   Stay behind with me, Addy. For just a little while.

ADELAIDE   I told the others to go on without me and when the last automobile had turned the corner, I sat down on the porch steps. The sun was shining, and it was so still you could hear the heartbeat of a bird. In the distance, I could see the Rockies.

They are as beautiful as Roger knew they would be. And the light... the light was so brilliant and clear that every pebble, and every leaf looked as if it had just been created.

I sat there for an hour and, George, Roger was with me. "Roger, I wish you could have seen..."

ROGER   I wish I could have seen, to, Addy. There is so much I wish I could have seen...

Adelaide turns to face him.

ADELAIDE   It's time to say goodbye, isn't it?

ROGER   It's time.

ADELAIDE   It never gets easy, but it's better if you keep it simple...

ROGER   Thank you Addy ... Goodbye.

ADELAIDE   Goodbye, Roger.

Roger walks away.

Suddenly the pain I felt since we left Saskatoon was gone. For the first time since Roger died, I was at peace.

My mind can't take this in, George, but in my heart I know that something is finished — no not finished, complete. Tonight I know that the circle is complete.

Lights up on George.

GEORGE   I have a gift for you, Addy. I've learned my first word in Greek — *'Eiréne*. It means 'peace'.

When you get to Vancouver, I want you to wade out into the Pacific and say, *'Eiréne'*. It'll be a kind of tribute to the members past and present, of the Blind and Halt Platoon from Saskatoon.

Lights down on George and up on Adelaide.

ADELAIDE   I'm here, George. I made it. "Halifax to Vancouver. Coast to coast, east to west, sea to shining sea..." Not shining yet... The sun still hasn't come up but I'm waiting, and I'm ready.

I brought the Snipe Lake medal. She looks at it ... "forged by McTaggart, polished by Currie..." The sky over the mountains is filling up with light.

Roger comes on stage, playing "The World is Waiting for the Sunrise" quietly on his harmonica. In the background the band joins him. The music becomes louder and more upbeat as the light on Addy becomes more intense.

ADELAIDE *looks at the medal and reads*   "... awarded to the all-Canadian euchre champion, the girl who got the 20th century off to the right start."

Well, let's hope. Let's hope.

Adelaide moves slowly in a circle, a movement suggestive of Roger's vision of her dancing in poppies.

ADELAIDE   *'Eiréne ... 'Eiréne ... 'Eiréne...*

Then she throws the medal in the air and George catches it.

ROGER/OUT *to the audience. During his speech, George and Adelaide's actions reflect his words.*

Nothing has an ending. There is no final note. We come into the light. We listen for our music. We reach out to one

PHOTO BY LAURENT ROY, SOHO PHOTOGRAPHY
PHOTO COURTESY OF GLOBE THEATRE AND THE SASKATCHEWAN ARCHIVES BOARD

Burgandy Code as Adelaide Farlinger

another and then, for a moment which is all eternity to us but a blink of the eye to God, we dance. We dance until our ears no longer hear the music, and the shadows gather us into the darkness.

New dancers have taken our place. You have taken our place. As you come into the light, as you listen for your music, remember us. Remember the horror of our lessons. Remember the beauty of our dance.

— THE END —